SEARCH THE SCRIPTURES

For the Words of Wisdom found therein

VOLUME TWO

YOU SHALL KNOW THE TRUTH

BENJAMIN BARUCH

Other books by Benjamin Baruch

The Day of the LORD is at Hand, 7th Edition

SEARCH THE SCRIPTURES

Volume One: Out of the Darkness

SEARCH THE SCRIPTURES

Volume Two
YOU SHALL KNOW THE TRUTH

Benjamin Baruch

First Edition April 21st, 2015

Printed in the United States of America

ISBN-13: 978-1511799379 ISBN-10: 1511799374

Underlining and other emphasis within the Scripture is the author's own. The author has translated certain scripture references into modern English for the benefit of the reader.

Look for the author's first book, ***The Day of the LORD is at Hand, Seventh Edition*** for insight into the prophetic writings, and for understanding of what is coming upon America and her church. You may also be blessed by the other books in the ***Search the Scriptures*** series including ***Volume One: Out of the Darkness.***

You may find other teaching materials & resources by Benjamin Baruch at: www.BenjaminBaruch.net

Dedication

I wish to dedicate this second volume of *Search the Scriptures, You Shall Know the Truth* to my Heavenly Father, who having blessed His remnant with all spiritual blessings in our Lord Jesus Christ, has chosen us and given unto us the greatest of honors, He adopted us as His own.

Blessed be the God and Father of our Lord Jesus Christ, who hath blessed us with all spiritual blessings in heavenly places in Christ: According as he hath chosen us in him before the foundation of the world, that we should be holy and without blame before him in love: Having predestinated us unto the adoption of children by Jesus Christ to himself, according to the good pleasure of his will, To the praise of the glory of his grace, wherein he hath made us accepted in the beloved.

Ephesians 1:3-6

For whatsoever is born of God overcometh the world: and this is the victory that overcometh the world, even our faith. Who is he that overcometh the world, but he that believeth that Jesus is the Son of God? This is he that came by water and blood, even Jesus Christ; not by water only, but by water and blood. And it is the Spirit that beareth witness, because the Spirit is truth. For there are three that bear record in heaven, the Father, the Word, and the Holy Ghost: and these three are one.

1st John 5:4-7

SEARCH THE SCRIPTURES

Volume Two:
YOU SHALL KNOW THE TRUTH

TABLE OF CONTENTS

Job

Let this sink into your hearts, the Son of Man shall be delivered into the hands of evil men, but they understood not this saying, for it was hidden from them so that they perceived it not.
Luke 9:44-45

All prophetic Scripture is fulfilled twice, for every word of God must be fulfilled twice, as the Scriptures declare: "God speaks once, yes twice, yet man perceives it not."[1] This must be so, for every word can only be established as the truth by the confirmation of two or more witnesses. Even the word of God is subject to this requirement. Thus, the Lord brings his word to pass twice, and it is fulfilled twice, and as it comes to pass, the day declares it to be so. God speaks once, and then his word is fulfilled twice, yet man perceives it not.

God told Adam, in the day he ate the fruit of the knowledge of good and evil, he would die, and Adam did die, twice. First, he died spiritually, and then later, he died in the flesh as well. God promised a messiah would come, and he did come, 2,000 years ago, and now he is coming again, for he comes twice. All the promises of God were spoken as one word, yet his word must always be fulfilled, and come to pass, twice. When the Lord Jesus Christ speaks prophetically, his words are also fulfilled twice, for he is the Word of God, and therefore, the Lord's own prophetic statements must also, always come to pass twice.

THEY PERCEIVED IT NOT, FOR IT WAS HIDDEN FROM THEM

The Lord spoke to the apostles about his soon arrest, persecution, and imminent crucifixion. He told them, let this sink down into your hearts, and understand what I am telling you, for the son of man shall be delivered into the hands of evil men, but they did not understand, because they did not want to understand. It was hidden from them, because they could not imagine that the Lord himself would be arrested, that he would be beaten, tortured and then crucified, and thus, they were unable to perceive his word. Looking back at the history of the nation of Israel, and the church within the New Covenant, this has always been true. Throughout all of time, the people to whom the word of God had come, could not comprehend or perceive the word. It was only after that generation perished, that a later generation would look back and understand.

This is true to this day regarding the book of Job, for many people are simply unable to perceive the word of the Lord as revealed, for they do not want to understand, and therefore, the meaning is hidden from them and "so they perceive it not."

THE BOOKS OF WISDOM

The book of Job is presented to us in the Scriptures immediately before the Psalms and the Proverbs, which are the books of wisdom. Job is counted among the books of wisdom, for its pages reveal a mystery of the very work and plan of God. In the story of Job's life, God uncovers a mystery of his kingdom and the work that he does, which he calls "*his strange work*" wherein he brings to pass, *"his strange act."* God has chosen to unveil this work through the life of Job, but it is a *"strange work"* and thus, we perceive it not, because it is absolutely incomprehensible to the many, therefore, its meaning has been hidden from us and we have perceived it not.

THERE WAS A MAN WHOSE NAME WAS JOB

There was a man in the land of Uz, whose name was Job; and that man was perfect and upright, and one that feared God, and eschewed evil. Job 1:1

The name *Job* is אִיּוֹב', *îyob* in Hebrew, and it means; a hated or persecuted one. The names given by God to his creation reveal the purposes, destiny, or gifting, given to them, and Job's name reveals who he was, for Job was a man who was hated in his time. All who desire to live righteously shall be persecuted and Job was living righteously in an unrighteous age, therefore, his name reveals the hatred and the persecution that he received from the fallen world around him.

The Scripture tells us Job was *perfect,* and the word used is תָּם , *tawm* which means to be complete and gentle, perfect and undefiled, and one who walks upright before the Lord. Job walked undefiled before the Lord. He was upright, and he also was a gentle man. He was not harsh and hard, and he was not cruel and critical. He was kind and considerate, unlike our generation, where the best among us, or rather the ones who think they are the most upright, are sharper than a thorn hedge, and are cruel and harsh in the dark counsel of their religious minds, yet they perceive it not.

Job was *upright,* and the word used is יָשָׁר, *yâshâr* which means he was just, righteous, and walked the straight path. He lived his life within the narrow way and he was one that feared God. The word for *feared* is יָרֵא, *yârê*[1] which means to be reverent, for he was morally fearful and reverent before God, and so he rejected evil. The Scripture declares, "this man was the greatest of all the men of the east."[2] The word for *greatest* is גָּדוֹל , *gâdôl* which means exceedingly great, noble and mighty and the word for *East* is קֶדֶם, *qedem* which means the time of antiquity, the time that was before, or the ancient times. The Scripture is telling us Job was the greatest of all the sons of men in the ancient times. He was the one man, who stood out from God's perspective, and he stood head and shoulders above every other man on the planet, for Job walked with the Lord. Job worshiped the Lord, and in his life, Job honored the Lord. In the ancient times, the Lord had one man who walked before him, in whom he was well pleased and that man's name was Job.

Job was also a faithful father. He would rise early to offer sacrifice to the Lord; peradventure his sons and daughters may have sinned in their hearts. From this we know that Job was an intercessor, a man who could be found standing in the gap for even the potential sins of his family. Job would rise early and present offerings and intercede before the Lord, and would stand and intercede for his children, for they might have sinned and cursed God in their hearts. The word for *cursed* in this text is the word בָּרַךְ, *bârak* and it means; one who is cursed or one who commits treason against God or the kingdom. There is a lot of wisdom in the Scriptures, each individual word is full of revelation, for it is an amazing book.

HAVE YOU CONSIDERED MY SERVANT JOB

The book of Job reveals to us that all of the sons of God, the entire angelic host, appeared before the Lord, and Satan came among them. And the Lord said unto Satan, "Have you considered my servant Job, there is none like him in the earth, a perfect and an upright man."[3] The word for *none* in this verse is אין, *ayin* and it means; nothing, non-extent, nowhere, and not at all.

There is no one like Job in all the earth. We do not know the earth's population at the time, but there could have been one billion people on the earth, and the Lord singles Job out, and tells the host heaven, he is the one man, in all the earth, who is the most upright, and so much so, that there is no one to compare to him.

This is Job; the hated and persecuted one. There is no one like him, for in the eyes of God, he is perfect. The word for *perfect* means; he is complete, and undefiled. It is not that Job was not a sinner, only that he was a man who had already repented and had fully turned from all of his wicked ways. Now he served God with all of his heart, and God counted him as righteous.

And so the Lord points him out to the enemy, saying, "there is none like him in all the earth." And of course the enemy responded saying, "you bless him and protect him, and you've got a hedge around him. Let me touch him and then we will see what happens." And so the controversy begins.

THE CONTROVERSY BEGINS

The LORD said unto Satan, Behold, all that he has is in thy power; only upon his flesh put not forth thine hand. So, Satan went forth from the presence of the LORD. Job 1:12

Here we are shown a glimpse into the absolute sovereignty of God, for the attacks of the enemy in the life of Job could only come with the permission of the Almighty, for it was God, who in his infinite wisdom, permitted and ordered these events. And he was not merely proving a point to Satan, as we are going to see from the Scriptures, for there is much more going on here.

AND IT CAME TO PASS

So Satan went forth, "and there was a day when Job's sons and daughters were eating and drinking wine in their eldest brother's house."[4] The word used in the text for *there was* is הָיָה, *hâyah*, and it means; it came to pass. But this word is emphatic, and it means something huge came to pass, not just the time came to pass. It means a beacon or a sign, and this word can also be translated to mean it broke, it came to break, and it also means to fall, and to quit oneself, or to come to the end of one's self. It came to pass that Job was going to be broken, and then find the end of himself. God is about to take the most righteous man walking the earth, and bring him to the end of himself. And we are going to find out why, and it is utterly amazing.

Satan is then given permission to put his hand on everything that Job has, and four purging's immediately come forth from the spirit world. First, the Sabeans come and fall upon his servants and carry off one thousand oxen and donkeys. All of the servants, save one, are killed by the edge of the sword. This judgment would not be easily misunderstood, for the enemy had attacked Job. The Lord had let his hedge of protection down, and the enemy was permitted to attack through the gates. They carried off all of the oxen and donkeys and killed the servants who were tending his flock, and while the first messenger was yet speaking, another messenger came running up to him, informing Job of the second purging. Fire had fallen from heaven, burning up the sheep of his pasture, and killing the servants who were tending them, consuming them as well.

The first purging could be attributed to the enemy, but the second appeared to be the very hand of God himself, falling from heaven, and not only did it destroy seven thousand sheep, it killed all the servants tending the sheep. We need to understand the context; this was the very flock that Job used to bring sacrifices to the Lord. Had the fire of God fallen from heaven when Job prepared a sacrifice on the altar, and had the fire of God come down upon the altar, that would have been interpreted as God accepting Job's sacrifice. That is what happened when Elijah prayed. Fire from heaven came down and consumed not only the altar but the water, everything. Fire falling on the altar would have been a sign of God's favor. The fact that the fire destroyed all seven thousand sheep, which were used in his religious worship of God, was interpreted as rejection by the Lord, and the most severe in history. No man had been rejected by fire from heaven before. There was nothing like this fire falling from heaven, in the history of the earth, and the only other example in Scripture is the burning of Sodom and Gomorrah.

The second purging gave the appearance that God had forsaken Job; for he must have done something to cause the Lord to be displeased to the point of literally judging Job's religious worship in the same manner in which he judged Sodom and Gomorrah. That news would have spread quickly through the entire land. "Did you hear what happened to Job?" And that was not the worst of the events of that day; for as Job was wrestling in his mind that perhaps God had become his enemy, another messenger appeared to inform Job of the third purging.

The Babylonians had come, stolen all of his camels, and killed his servants too. As Job was trying to absorb the fact that now all of his property was either stolen or burned in the fire, and all that he had was now destroyed, the fourth messenger arrived to give him the most severe news of all. A great wind from heaven had struck the house with his children inside, and not while they were praying, but while they were feasting in the flesh, and killed them all.

Job was now confronted with the ultimate sign of God's displeasure in his life. His children had died by a wind from heaven, and though this wind came by the hand of the enemy, for he is the prince of the power of the air, to anyone observing or hearing the report of these events, it appeared to be the hand of God and another token of his wrath. Not only were the sheep consumed with fire that fell similar to Sodom and Gomorrah, now Job's entire family had died while feasting. All of his children were now gone. The people would have thought, "they must have sinned and been cast away, because God only judges the wicked, while he blesses the righteous. He only brings his judgment upon the wicked." And these were some of the most severe judgments ever to fall upon a man.

Then Job arose, rent his mantle, and shaved his head, and fell down upon the ground, and worshipped God. Job 1:20

The word for *fell down* is נפל, *nâphal,* and it means; to fall, or to be cast down, to cease or to die, to fail and be judged, to be lost or overthrown, to be overwhelmed, to perish and be thrown down. And that is a clear picture of the state of the mind of Job, as these four incredible judgments fell upon him, giving the appearance that God had suddenly become Job's enemy, for everything he owned or loved had just been destroyed in one day. And so Job is overwhelmed and overthrown, and then, Job falls to the ground and worships God! And that word for *worship* in the text is שחה, *shaw-khaw,* and it means; to bow down before royalty and to humbly worship.

Job then speaks and says, "Naked came I out of my mother's womb, and naked shall I return thither: the Lord gave, and the Lord hath taken away; blessed be the name of the Lord." In all this, Job sinned not, nor charged God foolishly."[5] How many of us would respond to the loss of everything we own, and all of our children in a single day in this fashion? Yet this is how Job responded, and in all of this, Job sinned not, nor did he charge God foolishly.

The Scripture returns to the scene in heaven, and the sons of God again appear before the Lord with Satan also, and the Lord again says to Satan:

Hast thou considered my servant Job, that there is none like him in the earth, a perfect and an upright man, one that fears God, and eschews evil and still he holds fast his integrity, although thou moved me against him, to destroy him without cause. Job 2:3

Integrity means innocence and it is the word ת מ ה, *toom-maw.* God is saying, Job is innocent before me. And the Lord says to Satan, "you moved me to destroy him without cause." The word for *destroy* is ב ל ע, *baw-lah'* which means; to devour, to bring to an end, to swallow up, and to destroy. And the word for *without cause* is ח נ ם, *khin-nawm* which means; devoid of reason, without a cause, guiltless, innocent, for nothing, for not, in vain. God is declaring there was nothing Job did that caused God to allow this to happen, but the Lord did allow it. It was without cause, but it was not without a purpose.

The Lord does not do random, and he is not just having an argument with Satan. He is not just trying to prove a point. He did not kill Job's children (they did not stay dead, they went to heaven) and he did not burn down Job's house, and destroy all of Job's property, reducing Job to destitution and poverty just to make a point. There was a purpose and that purpose has a lot to do with the books of wisdom; it is the mystery of the purpose of God in all of us, for God does the same work in each of us. Do you understand yet? Do you yet perceive?

For the Son of Man must be delivered into the hands of evil men. Let this sink into your hearts. Yet to this day most people do not understand. You hear people all the time saying, "If God is good, why does he allow bad things to happen? If God is so good, why does he choose us in a furnace of affliction? If God is good, why did this happen to Job?" If Job was righteous, and there was no cause in Job, what was God's purpose in all this?

THE FINAL PURGING OF JOB

And the LORD said unto Satan, Hast thou considered my servant Job, that there is none like him in the earth, a perfect and an upright man, one that fears God, and eschews evil and still he holds fast his integrity, although thou moved me against him, to destroy[4] him without cause. Job 2:3

Satan responds, "Skin for skin yea, all that a man hath will he give for his life. But put forth thine hand now, and touch his bone and his flesh, and he will curse thee to thy face."[6] And so, the Lord grants Satan the authority to *touch* Job.

And the LORD said unto Satan, Behold, he is in thine hand; but save his life. So went Satan forth from the presence of the LORD, and smote Job with sore boils from the sole of his foot unto his crown. Job 2:6-7

God then grants Satan permission to *touch* the life of Job, but he is not permitted to take Job's life. "You can take everything else, but do not take his life." God does not afflict the sons of men willingly. The Lord does not discipline, afflict and purge his children just because he can do it, even as we do not spank our children just because we can do it. But the Lord will use the furnace of affliction to bring us to righteousness.

In this generation, people do not understand these things because the modern American version of Christianity does not really have a cross involved. They want all the blessings without the power of the cross, and in a lot of churches, they want the blessings of God, without repentance from sin either.

In order to receive the blessings from heaven, we have to repent of our sin, and we definitely need the power of the cross, without which we are going nowhere with the Lord other than wandering around in the wilderness of sin, and dying in that wilderness, without ever having entered in to the promises of God.

So, Satan went forth from the presence of the Lord and smote Job with sore boils from the soles of his feet, unto the crown of his head. And they were sore boils. So now we can picture what this was like for Job; his children have just been killed, all of his property has been stolen or burned, his house has been destroyed as well, and Job himself, is now covered in sore boils from head to toe. The word for *sore* used in the text is רעה, *raʿâh* and it means; evil, adversity, exceedingly grievous and heavy misery, wretchedness, and far worse than bad. The word for *boils* used in the text is שחין, *shᵉchîyn* and it means; a burning inflamed ulcer or boils: a broken open wound that burns exceedingly.

Job's entire body is now covered in burning, grievous and exceedingly wretched and inflamed ulcers. Think of chickenpox on steroids. Job had intense, burning and open ulcers all over his body. He could not stand, for they were on the bottom of his feet. He could not sit, because they were on the bottom of his seat. He could not do anything. He has lost everything, and now his health is removed. This man is in agony, as his life has been reduced to an utter desolation.

> *And he took him a potsherd to scrape himself withal; and he sat down among the ashes. Job 2:8*

Job takes a broken piece of pottery, from what once was his kitchen, a fragment of the fancy China his wife had always wanted, only now it was smashed into pieces and he sits down, among the ashes, to scrape himself. Let us look clearly at the picture of what is happening here. That word for *sat down* in the text is י שׁ ב, *yâ̂shab* and it means; to sit down and to dwell, to remain, and to make a home. He was home. He sat down in his house, which was now a burned-out pile of rubble, and started picking through the ashes for pieces of broken pottery to scrape the burning open sores which covered his body.

This is incomprehensible. It is simply unbelievable, and that is why we perceive it not. None of us have seen this in our own lives, save the anointed ones who have been appointed for this hour, who have all been chosen to walk in this same path. Some of us may have had a little taste of what Job went through, we may have lost a job, had some of our flock stolen, or we might even have lost a child. Perhaps we had chickenpox as an adult. But we did not lose our job and all of our property, our children and our health, and watch our house burn to rubble all on the same day.

Can you even imagine what this must have felt like to Job, for it all happened on the same day? So Job sits down, scraping his wounds, and begins to live in the ruins of what once was his house. Because where else would he go? So, he sits down and starts to live amidst the ashes of what was once his life. And all that was left for him were a few broken pieces of pottery, to scrape the burning ulcers that are oozing all over his body. So, there you have it. That was Job's purging, and now the real trial begins, because now, his religious friends are going to come and "help" him. And they mean well, but as we are going to see from the text, they do not do well at all.

> *Now when Job's three friends heard of all this evil that was come upon him, they came everyone from his own place; Eliphaz the Temanite, and Bildad the Shuhite, and Zophar the Naamathite: for they had made an appointment together to come to mourn with him and to comfort him. Job 2:11*

Just the physical affliction of Job would be enough to put most people over the edge, but Job has not complained to the Lord. He worshiped the Lord and gave thanks to the Lord for what at one time was his. He was a righteous man, and he kept his righteousness before God, and because of this, as we are going to see, he has a significant place in the prophetic picture of the word of God. He is actually a very important character from the Hall of Faith, and we will all meet him in the kingdom, if and when we get there.

Let us review what has happened in the life of Job thus far. This had to be big news, fire coming down from heaven and burning up seven thousand sheep. Just consider how much fire that had to be; seven thousand sheep do not just stand in perfect lines, they would have been scattered all over several hills. A huge firestorm fell from heaven, like the fire of Sodom and Gomorrah. People from all over the region would have seen this pillar of fire come down, and the smoke of the burning would have covered the skies. The people would have asked, "what was that?" "Oh, that was just the fire of God destroying everything Job did religiously." And they hated him already. His name meant hated and now they knew why. Now they had the goods on him, and so the people began to mock him. He became a proverb among the people. They sang songs about what a loser Job was. They slandered him up and down the countryside. His friends all abandoned him, for they esteemed him smitten and afflicted of God, so most of his friends would not even speak to him any longer.

We all pass through trials, but Job had a massive trial, for Job got it all. And the news traveled all around the ancient land in that region, because they would have seen those fires. This would have been front-page news in that day. "Did you hear what happened to Job? Everything he had was stolen or destroyed in the fire, and he, himself, covered in grievous boils. He looks like a leper, and he is living in the ashes of his burned-out house." People are laughing at him and making fun of him. He had become the butt of their jokes. They already hated him because his righteousness condemned them and now that he is down, they are kicking him. They considered him afflicted by God. It was fire from heaven and it must have been the wrath of God. The Almighty had rebuked this man who thought he was so good. Job acted righteously, and everyone else took that as a condemnation from him, so people wanted to get even with Job.

EVERYONE WHO LIVES GODLY SHALL BE PERSECUTED

Everyone who lives godly shall be persecuted, and so, Job is being slandered, mocked and forsaken. Unless you have been there, I do not think you can comprehend what goes through the mind of a man who has lost everything he loves, everything he owns, and then even his own flesh begins to burn within.

And in Job's mind, now he has Satan on his right hand, standing there to accuse him. "Job, maybe God did forsake you. Maybe there is something you just cannot see, something you are in denial of. Your heart is deceitfully wicked and the Lord might have found some wickedness in you. Job, to whom much is given, much is required, and the Lord gave you all of this and righteousness too. And now God has turned his back on you."

Job is in misery. He cannot sleep. He just lays there under the cold stars, for he does not have a blanket, it burned with everything else in the fire. He is lying in mud, because when the dew would come in the morning, the ashes would turn into mud. So, he is sleeping in the mud, with the smell of smoke all around him, staring up at the stars in utter agony from his burning sores, and he has the devil on his right hand telling him, "God has forsaken you" and all of the people in the surrounding villages mocking him.

Finally, Job's three remaining friends, when they heard of all of the evil that came upon him, made an appointment together, to come and to mourn with him, and to comfort him. Notice, they did not just drop what they were doing and run to help Job. They got out their calendars, and found a time that was convenient for them, and that is the sense implied here in the Scripture. When it was convenient, they made an appointment, like many Christians are with the Lord, when they can find a little spare time to fit God in, they do so. In like manner, Job's friends made an appointment to come and to mourn with him, and to comfort him. Their hearts were in the right place, and these were the only friends Job had left, for everyone else had forsaken him.

And when they lifted up their eyes afar off, and knew him not, they lifted up their voice, and wept; and they rent everyone his mantle, and sprinkled dust upon their heads toward heaven. Job 2:12

As they journeyed towards Job's property, they came upon his land and saw the ruins of where his house once stood. They saw a strange figure covered in boils, which no longer even looked like a man, his appearance was marred more than any man, and they lifted up their eyes from far off but they knew him not. They could not even recognize him. He did not look like the Job they knew. He was just one big boil, from the top of his head to the bottom of his feet, and they were oozing and burning. Can you imagine? He would have had them in his mouth, even in his throat. This man is going through the full Monty and his closest friends could not even recognize him.

When they realize it was their friend Job, they lifted up their voices and wept, and every one of them tore their garments, and threw dust and ashes on their heads. They came to Job and saw him sitting in the ashes, and they sat down with him on the ground for seven days and seven nights. It does not say they ate anything. Job, no doubt, is fasting at this point. He cannot eat because he has boils in his throat. Job does not even know what has happened to him. He thought he was doing the right thing before the Lord, but now everything has been destroyed. Everyone has forsaken him and Satan is now accusing him night and day. He is beginning to wonder if maybe, somehow, God has become his enemy. So, he is sitting there waiting on God in absolute torment, and in utter misery. His friends then sit down with him, and for seven days and seven nights, and they do not speak a word.

The seven days and seven nights represent a prophetic picture of the seven years of tribulation that are coming upon the world at the end of the age. Seven years of hardships are coming. But his friends would not even speak a word, for they saw his grief was very great.

The Scripture tells us, "every one of them came from his own place." And that word for *own place* in the text is מָקוֹם, *māqôm* and it means, from where they stood, from their location but it also means from the condition of their mind. They came to help Job, but they came from the place of their own understanding, and they came in the mind of the flesh. They came with their knowledge of good and evil and with the best of intentions, to help their friend. But, as we are going to see, very quickly that changes, because they are going to stand up in pride when they judge Job and after Job tells them they are wrong, they are going to get offended with him and are going to become his accusers. His only remaining friends, who have come to comfort him, now become his accusers. Think about this scenario; this man has been completely annihilated. God said, "I destroyed him" and his three best friends, the only friends he has left, now become his accusers. Then they begin to judge and mock him just as Jesus, himself, would centuries later be mocked on the cross.

A MAN CHILD IS CONCEIVED

After the seven days of mourning, Job opens his mouth and begins to speak and he curses his day. Job began to say, "Let the day perish wherein I was born and the night in which it was said there is a man child conceived."[7] This statement by Job is the first prophetic clue that there is more going on here than simply a severe trial of a man of God, for the word for *man-child* used in this text is גֶּבֶר, *gheber*, and *gheber* does not mean a little child or a male child. The word for *male child* in Hebrew is ילד, *yeled*, but here Job says *gheber*, which means a valiant man, or a warrior has been born.

On the night when they said "there has been a warrior conceived." A valiant man of faith and a warrior of God has been born into the earth and look what he went through to be prepared. The purging of Job is a picture of the refining fires that God brings into the life of the man child of the book of Revelation. God put Job through the furnace. The ministry of the *man child* of the book of Revelation is the ministry of the 144,000, who are pictured standing with the Lord on Mount Zion, for their lives are part of the ministry of Jesus Christ. They are going to walk out the second half of the ministry of Jesus Christ on the earth. If you can receive it, the Scripture clearly declares, Jesus Christ has a seven-year ministry on the earth. He did the first half himself when he came as a man, and now he is going to do the second half himself as God, operating through an anointed remnant of men that have been totally sanctified by the furnace of affliction much like the life of Job.

The life of Job is a picture of the furnace. The ministry of Jesus Christ is the ministry of the Messiah who confirms the covenant that his Father made with Abraham, Isaac and Jacob, and all of true Israel, including all of the Gentiles who would be called, chosen and also grafted in. God made a covenant with his people, and he sent his son, Jesus, to fulfill it. We did not save ourselves, Jesus saved us. We know from the prophecy in the book of Daniel, that the Messiah will confirm the covenant for "seven years." He comes and fulfills all of the righteous requirements of the covenant. He completed the first 3 ½ years of his ministry himself, as a man, 2000 years ago. Everyone understands that part. He was crucified and died for the sins of his people, and then, he rose again.

If you can receive it, what Jesus went through when he was arrested on the night of the Passover, was a far greater purging. He was beaten and chained, and then they tortured him, put a crown of thorns upon his head, and hit him with pieces of wood in the face. They scourged him with whips that tore the flesh off his back, and made him carry a cross, which must have weighed a ton, up to Calvary's hill. There they pounded nails into his hands and his feet, and left him to die on the cross for our sins; all of that happened in the space of one day.

From the night he was arrested, to the scourging the next day, to the crucifixion, that afternoon, all of it occurred in a single day. What happened to Job was far less than what the Lord endured. Job only had a taste of the cup that Jesus drank from. Is it not right that the servant should drink the same cup as the Master? At least taste something of what the Master would endure. We were saved by the cross, but Jesus had to pay the price.

What does God require of us? Only that we repent from being so self-centered, and learn to love one another, stop hurting each other, start living righteously, maybe even fast and pray a little. What did God require of Jesus? He required the cross. What did he require of Job? He required Job to be a type and a shadow of what Jesus would suffer, for like Job, the Lord had everything taken from him in one day, including his life. Most of the Lord's friends all forsook him when he was arrested, and some even betrayed him. Only John, Mary and his mother stood with him in the hour of his suffering. One of his closest friends, became a traitor to him. Job represents a type and shadow of what God himself would endure in the fire of the cross.

The ministry of Jesus Christ is seven years. My authority for this is Daniel chapter 9:24-27. "He shall confirm the covenant with the many for one week." In the midst of the seven years, he will cause the offering and a sacrifice to cease. All the modern prophecy teachers have told you, the 70th week of Daniel is the final seven years of tribulation upon the earth, and the time in which the antichrist confirms the covenant of death which Israel has made with her enemies in the last days. The last part is true, but it is not the true fulfillment of this prophecy, but merely a counterfeit fulfillment.

Remember, every prophetic word must be fulfilled twice, for the true Messiah, Jesus Christ, also fulfills the true covenant made by his Father with his people. The ministry of Jesus Christ, which is a seven-year ministry, is the true fulfillment of the true covenant. The false Messiah is merely confirming the false covenant, the covenant of death spoken of in Isaiah 28.

The ministry of the Messiah is to confirm the true covenant for seven years and in the midst of his seven year ministry, the sacrifices would be stopped. After Jesus died on the cross, and completed the first three and half years of his ministry, the sacrifice of the Temple was stopped, and the entire old covenant sacrificial system was destroyed and canceled when the Romans came and burned the Temple to the ground. There has not been a sacrifice or a Temple since that time. But the Lord is not finished with his seven-year ministry in confirming his covenant.

A pastor friend of mine once said to me, "I am having a hard time understanding that Jesus would have a seven-year ministry on the earth." I responded, "Well, that is his number, right? Seven is the perfect number of God. Does it not make sense that the ministry of the Messiah in confirming the perfect covenant would also be a seven-year period?" The Lord has a seven-year ministry. This is clearly declared in the Scriptures. But once again the people perceive it not. Now, I know this to be true, because I was in my home many years ago, and the Lord began to speak to me and said, "I have a seven-year ministry on the earth and I am only half finished." I thought, "Really? I have never heard that before."

The life of Job is a picture of part of this ministry, and this is why. What is the very center point of the ministry of Jesus Christ in fulfilling the covenant of God unto our salvation? What is at the very center of the ministry of Jesus Christ? What is lifted up on the high hill, as the means by which the bond of the covenant is fulfilled and confirmed? And what is the power through which we are saved and delivered? It is the cross! It is the blood of the covenant through Christ's death on the cross that stands at the very center of eternity.

The cross of Jesus Christ is the dividing line of eternal time, because on that day, God Almighty died. Of course, he did not stay dead, because even though they killed him in the flesh, and he died as a man, yet he is God, and thus he rose from the dead.

The ministry of Jesus Christ is seven years. He did the first half himself as a man, 2,000 years ago. Even though he is God, he came among us a man and as the Lamb of God. He is about to come among us again, only this time as the Lion of Judah, to complete the second half of his seven year ministry, during the time of the Great Tribulation. Before he comes as the King of Kings, in the clouds, he is going to first come in an anointed remnant of his people, revealing himself as the Lion from Judah. The idea of Christ in you as the hope of glory is not a new idea, for the Scripture is clear that God will come in us, his new and living Temple, which has been made without hands.

These Bible verses we have all learned and quoted are going to be fulfilled as an objective reality, and not something to be merely apprehended in the spirit. Rather, they shall all be literally fulfilled in the earth, in the last days. These promises will become a reality in the lives of the sanctified and redeemed ones. An anointed remnant is going to fulfill and walk out the ministry of Jesus Christ when he comes to be revealed among us through the power of God in the spirit. Jesus Christ is going to come, first through the Holy Spirit in which 144,000 men are going to be completely born again and totally purified.

They are not superstars; they are actually of the lowliest ones among us and they know they are nothing without the Lord. They are chosen by the Lord for this reason, because they are not going to get in the way of what he wants to do in the earth. They understand, this is the ministry of Jesus Christ, and not their ministry at all. They only came to serve the Lord and they are merely the vessels of his glory, which he has prepared for the deliverance of his people.

Jesus ministered as a man for 3 ½ years, and he completed his ministry as the Lamb of God at the cross, with his death and resurrection. He then appeared to the disciples for 40 days, but the work of his ministry as a man ended at the cross. His ministry as the Lamb of God was completed when he said on the cross, "it is finished." So then, the ministry of the 144,000 must begin at the cross. Jesus starts the second half of his ministry right where he left off, at the cross.

What Job endured is a picture of the cross that each of the 144,000 will ultimately walk through, in one form or another. That is why Job said, "on the night that a man child was conceived." A valiant warrior has been ordained to be born into the earth, and before he can be used as an instrument of Jesus Christ for the fulfillment of his ministry, the men who have been chosen by God as part of this company, who are the first fruits of the resurrection of Jesus Christ, must endure a cross of their own. Before they are given the incredible blessing to become part of the ministry of Jesus Christ, he is first going to take them to the cross. They have to become crucified to their flesh. They must die to themselves completely. There cannot be anything left of the soul of the carnal mind or the knowledge of good and evil to get in the way of the ministry of Jesus Christ.

Do you yet perceive this, dear reader; can you comprehend these mysteries of the kingdom? The confirmation of the Covenant of Death by the antichrist is nothing more than another counterfeit of the ministry of the true Messiah, Jesus Christ, who comes to confirm the True Covenant for seven years. Satan has never had an original idea throughout eternity; everything he does is only a counterfeit. And now, as the Lord is about to fulfill the second half of his seven-year ministry, he is preparing the vessels of his own choosing, first burning them in the fires of affliction and reducing their lives to ashes, much like he reduced Job to ashes through the furnace of his affliction.

I have grown to love the furnace of affliction, though not for the pain. I never have and I never will enjoy the pain, but I love the holiness that is worked within you. You come out the other side different and it is utterly amazing. Job was taken to the point of total desolation, for God actually destroyed the life of Job. The Lord says as much himself in the Scriptures, "I destroyed him."

Some who do not understand these mysteries have taught all of this came upon Job because of fear, for at one point Job makes the statement, "that which I feared has come upon me." This is a popular teaching today regarding the book of Job, but the Lord already told us, "I did this without cause." Job was more righteous than any of us. In many places in the Scriptures, when the Lord talks about the judgment coming upon the earth, he makes the statement, "if Noah or Daniel or Job was standing among them, they would only save themselves." Job is in the company of Noah and Daniel; he stands among the elite of God's elect Saints. God did not destroy the life of Job simply because he had a slight fear in his heart and the Lord tells us clearly, "I did it without cause."

There was nothing in Job that caused God to destroy him, but there was a purpose, and the purpose was to bring Job to a place which Job had never seen before. Job was righteous and walked upright before the Lord, as righteous as a man in the flesh could ever be. If Job had his life annihilated because of a small defect in him, and none of us are without sin, then every one of us can expect the treatment that Job received. And most of us never see anything like this in our lives. Most believers will never experience the trial by fire that occurred in Job's life. It was because there was something that was not yet in Job, that Father God wanted to work into Job's character, and it could only occur in the fires of affliction. We all go through trials and tribulation, because he that has suffered has ceased from sin.

The Scripture teaches us that even Jesus Christ learned obedience through the things which he suffered, so the trials, persecutions and the tribulations of this life are one of the ways Father God teaches us obedience and righteousness. Job experienced this at the ultimate level. When Job made the statement that *a man-child* had been conceived, and a mighty warrior had come, he was prophesying of the anointed ones who could come at the time of the end, only they must first walk in his shoes as their lives are reduced to ashes as well.

In Isaiah 8:18, the Scripture says, "Behold, I and the children whom the Lord has given are for signs and wonders in the land of Israel." And the word used for *"I"* in this text is the *royal "I"*. This is the King who is speaking, and he speaks of himself and of the man-child company whom Father God has given. The English Bibles all say "given me" in this text, but the word for *me* is not in the Hebrew, it was added to the English translation.

THE MINISTRY OF JESUS CHRIST

This is Jesus Christ who is speaking, saying *"Behold,* look and see, open your eyes and see, I, the Messiah, and the man-child company, who are my valiant and anointed warriors, chosen by my Father, and were given by God to Israel, for signs and wonders in the land." Now the man-child company, who are the 144,000, are mere men. Jesus Christ was also a man, but he was not just a man, no, he was and is, God Almighty. He is the very Son of God, so even though he came as a man, he was God in the flesh. But the man-child company, they are just men, until the spirit of God Almighty comes upon them without measure, and then they too will become vessels who are filled to overflowing, and they will become the Princes in Israel who will rule in the hour of judgment that is coming during the Great Tribulation.

This mystery is revealed in the following prophecy: "Behold, a king shall reign in righteousness, and his princes shall rule in judgment."[8] The man-child company is the army of God. They are the mighty ones whom the Lord has called.

> *I have commanded my sanctified ones; I have also called my mighty ones for my anger, even them that rejoice in my highness. The noise of a multitude in the mountains, like as of a great people; a tumultuous noise of the kingdoms of nations gathered together: the Lord of hosts musters the host of the battle. They come from a far country, from the end of heaven, even the Lord, and they are the weapons of his indignation, to destroy the whole land. Howl ye; for the day of the LORD is at hand. Isaiah 13:2-6*

They first come as the Lord's Sheriff department and they perform search and rescue missions for the children of God who are lost, and then they will be revealed as the military arm of the kingdom of God, for they will wage war for the Lord and ultimately overturn the kingdom of the beast.

Our God is a King, and he has a kingdom, and in his kingdom, he has a family, a people that he loves, for his subjects are actually his family. He is the King in his house, and he has people of all sorts; little boys, and little girls, young men, vessels of honor, and he fashions them for worship and for holding his glory. He has pastors, teachers, and evangelists, but he also has an army. He has men of war that he has prepared for fighting, and not everyone is in the military.

He can fashion us to be whatever type of vessel he chooses. He makes out of the same clay one vessel and then another. He makes one a vessel of honor, another, a vessel of dishonor. He makes vessels of worship, but he also makes weapons of war. A cup is used for rejoicing in his house. If he fashions you as a cup, he starts with clay, then he adds living water, and then you need some heat, so you are going to have a little trial and tribulation. God is going to turn the heat up, and then he is going to mold you in his hands. He is going to shape you into a beautiful cup. Then he will place the cup back into the furnace to sear and harden the cup into the beautiful form that it is. Then he is going to glaze it over and it will become a beautiful goblet in the hand of the Lord. Then the Lord is going to say, "That is mine, and I will use this cup for rejoicing. I made this vessel to worship before me and to be filled with my joy and to sing forth my praises." He sets it at his right hand and says, "That one is mine, and maybe I'll put a few jewels in it too."

Then the Lord says, "I have a war coming, and I am going to have to fight my old enemy, and it is going to be the final conflict. So, I am going to raise an army, and I am going to fashion myself weapons of war."

This time he does not start with clay, for it would not work well as a sword. Instead, he reaches down into the earth and he pulls out iron ore. "I am not making a cup; I need a sword for this job." So, he takes the purest iron ore he can find and heats it up, but he does not heat it like you would heat clay in pottery class. No, he has to first melt the iron ore, so instead of 200°, he uses a blast furnace at 6000°. Instead of molding it with his hands, God gets out his sledgehammer. He pounds the sword and if it is going to be a two edged sword and razor-sharp, how many blows will it need? How hot will the furnace need to be and how pure must the instrument become?

If there is a slight imperfection in the clay, the cup will still work fine for rejoicing; but any defect in the sword, and it will break in battle. So, the sword must become perfectly purified, which is what we all become when we enter the new Kingdom and receive our new bodies, but we are talking about the ministry for which the 144,000 were called in this present hour.

The Lord speaks of them in the prophecy of Isaiah 13 saying, "I have commanded my sanctified ones" for they have been purified totally, in a furnace like Job. The life of Job is a picture of the preparation of the 144,000 and of the blast furnace God uses to fashion his weapons of war. Isaiah continues saying, "I have called my mighty ones" and the word in this text for *mighty* means, champions, and warriors. This is God's Delta force and they are a serious group of people. The Lord put them through some serious preparations, and they are going to do some serious business for the King, because they are going to be used by God as weapons of warfare, as we shall see. Isaiah continues, "I have called my mighty ones for my anger."

In the Hebrew, the word for *anger* is זעם, *zah'-am* and it means; fury, indignation, anger and rage. Their ministry is the anger of the Lord, and they rejoice in lifting his name up. For their ministry is not to exalt themselves, but the Lord. In verse four, the Scripture declares, "the Lord of hosts gathers together his army for the battle." These are not women and children, these are men of war. In verse five we are told, "They come from a far country, from the end of heaven" and who could come from heaven? The Scripture tells us the answer, "even the Lord." So it is the Lord in these men and who are they? They are the weapons of his indignation, and they come to destroy the whole earth. They will bring the final judgment upon the whole world. Theirs is an interesting ministry, don't you think? And what do they do? They first deliver God's saints from the battle that is going to take place in the Great Tribulation, and then, they are sent back to deal with the kingdom of darkness. In Isaiah 13:6 the Scriptures declare the hour of their ministry, "Howl ye, for the day of the Lord is at hand."

The life of Job is a picture of the fires of preparation the Lord puts his anointed ones through that have been called to this special purpose. God put Job through the same process and Job's reference to a "man-child" having been born is a prophetic picture of the preparation of the man-child company and the sacrifice of Jesus Christ. It is a picture of the price the Lord paid, for the suffering of Lord cannot even be quantified. If you have never been in the blast furnace of the Lord, where you learn the real meaning of the word, *suffering,* then you cannot even imagine it. Some saints walk through this kind of fire. The martyrs go through this fire. In the case of Job, his time in the furnace of affliction went on for months.

We do not know how long Job's furnace burned, and how long this experience lasted for him, but we do know from the Scripture that it was months long at a minimum. As Job begins praying in chapter 3, not only does he tell you about the birth of the man-child, but after, he reveals the events of the Great Tribulation which are going to take place as soon as the man-child is born.

In chapter 3, Job declares, "let the day perish when the man child is born." When the man-child of the book of Revelation is born, then a time such as never was, shall begin. Jesus referred to this in Luke 17 when he said, "on the day you see the Son of Man revealed, do not even go back into your house for then there shall be days of tribulation such as have never been." On the day the Son of Man is revealed, when the man-child of the book of Revelation will be revealed, and when Jesus Christ is revealed within the remnant of his people, the Great Tribulation shall begin. In the account given in Matthew 24, the Lord says, "when you see the abomination of desolation." This is the event which marks the beginning of the Great Tribulation, while in the account in Luke, the Lord does not mention the abomination of desolation, rather he says, "on the day you see the Son of Man revealed." Therefore, both occur on the same day.

The man-child company must first pass through the cross and the fires of purification before they can begin their ministry. God has to completely empty them of themselves, so they will not get in the way of the work the Lord wants to do, because he is going to use their lives for the revealing of the Son of Man. Christ in all of us, the hope of glory. Why this is not commonly understood within the church is beyond me, because this is the revelation of Jesus Christ. One of the reasons, I suppose, is that much of the church believes they are simply going to disappear before the tribulation even comes.

Other people, even entire denominations, claim that they are the 144,000. If the truth be told, you might not want to be among this company of men, because of the suffering they had to endure, and the price they had to pay, even unto their very lives being lost. During the Great Tribulation, they will be the mighty ones of God, and beyond the reach of the Dragon, but this is the military, and would you really have wanted to join the Army?

You first have to go through Boot Camp and then Ranger training. Then you must be trained in Special Forces operations and you have to go through Delta force training, and then survive the Navy Seal program. Is that what you want to do? That is who these guys are, and that is a picture of the fire through which they have walked. It cost them everything to be in this company of men. They have lived lives that can be best pictured by the life of Job, for everything that they had and everything that they were, the Lord burned utterly in the fire.

The level of pain and suffering which they have endured is beyond the comprehension of the many who will be delivered by this company of men. This is the Lord's Navy Seal unit, and these guys are hard-core. They have been through some hard-core preparations. I do not think you get to volunteer for this job; you get drafted by the Lord for this one. And I do not think the Lord asked any of them, "would you like to be part of my army?"

The suffering of Job is also a picture of the process of redemption, for the Lord uses the fires of affliction to bring us to righteousness, particularly when we refuse to voluntarily cooperate in the process of sanctification. God literally burns the sin and the pride right out of us. God is using the Great Tribulation and the persecution of this life, which has been here from the beginning. Job's name means "persecuted", so God has been using the furnace of affliction from the very beginning, to bring his saints to a place of total repentance, for some things can only be understood through suffering.

The knowledge of good and evil within each of us only causes us to become religious. We become critical, and judgmental, and full of pride; and when we are in that state of mind, filled with our pride, we are not going to listen to anyone, because we already know everything. We are going to see this from Job's friends in a moment. The Scripture says the instruction of a fool is folly, for those who are lost in a mind filled with pride, have become fools, so to try to instruct them is only folly. It is not going to work. But the Scripture also says, "the rod is prepared for the back of the fool." So when God brings the affliction, then we finally get rid of that attitude and then we all learn to humble ourselves.

Pride is so deceitful; you can have pride and not even know you have it. The human heart is deceitful, above all things. We could be walking in pride and rebellion, and all the while, thinking we are engaged in ministry. That is why the Lord must afflict the children of men. And that is why when God commands us to fast and pray in this hour, if we do not want to cooperate and follow the Lord's instructions, we give him no other choice but to do the work in us through fire. And to varying degrees, depending on how stubborn and strong-willed we are, or depending on how arrogant and proud we are, or how brainwashed and deceived we are, God uses affliction and tribulation in every one of our lives.

God said, "I chose you in the furnace of affliction." He does not put you there, he chose you there and God keeps the heat on until all of the impurities are removed. He knows when you are pure; it is when he can see his own image in you, uncorrupted by the dark counsel of this wicked age, and no longer mixed with the sins of the lust of the flesh and the pride of this life.

> *Confirming the souls of the disciples, and exhorting them to continue in the faith, and that we must through much tribulation enter into the kingdom of God. Acts14:22*

We live amongst the generation of his wrath, for in these last days, a great apostasy has come. The people have turned from the truth and are no longer willing to receive sound doctrine, rather they follow doctrines from the imaginations of the mind of men, doctrines of devils, and many of them are following them straight into hell. Even among the remnant, who are appointed unto salvation, there are so few who are actually overcoming the world, the flesh and the devil. It is only through the things that we suffer, that we actually learn obedience unto righteousness. God offers us fasting and prayer as an alternative, but not many of us choose to obey, and are willing to fast and pray. That leaves the only other alternative, the furnace of affliction.

Fasting and prayer is actually much more comfortable than the furnace of affliction, but you have to do it to do it. And in this hour, practically no one wants to do the prayer and fasting which is required to break down the strongholds of the evil one in their lives. Jesus told us, some things can only be broken through fasting and prayer. The tribulation that is coming, it will be more than adequate to get the job done in all of us. The good news is, God does not forsake us in the furnace of affliction, rather he walks with us, right through it, like he walked with the Hebrew boys in the furnace of Babylon. None of us want to suffer, and we do not choose that path willingly, but the truth is, we only learn patience and obedience through the fires of affliction. The Scripture tells us, we are to glorify the Lord in the fires, and when the fire of affliction has purified our hearts, we will be able to worship God and give thanks in the midst of the affliction, because we will be able to perceive through the eyes of faith the wonderful work of righteousness which he is working within us, and that we are nearing the end of God's strange work in our lives.

The furnace of affliction completely empties you of yourself. In most churches today, the majority of believers are still walking in the flesh, and they are still subject to the dark counsel of this present fallen age. It continues to influence their ways of thinking and it continues to dominate their emotional responses to the events in their lives, such that many bring only an offering of strife and contention in the house of God. The Lord spoke to me regarding the condition of the many within the church saying, "My people are full of themselves, but I will empty them out." It is within the furnaces of affliction that we get emptied out.

So, let us turn our focus back to Job and his time in the furnace of affliction. And bear in mind, God chose to do this work in the most righteous man of that generation. God did not do this work in people that were walking in compromise; he did this in the man that he was most impressed with. The Lord held Job in very high esteem. God even brags about him before the host of heaven. God had looked upon the earth, and he saw every man doing what was right in his own eyes, and all of them, altogether worthless. Every table was full of vomit, and every heart full of sin and compromise within, such was the state of all mankind. Then there was Job, the one man whose heart was right before God. And God chose him, to be brought to the end of himself, through the furnaces of affliction. God saw one man standing alone, and he chose to do a work in him that you are not going to believe even if it is told to you, and it is good what God did in Job. And Job got blessed in the process; everything was restored unto him in the end, even a double portion from the Lord.

THE KNOWLEDGE OF GOOD AND EVIL

But before the work could be finished, after the fires went out, Job needed to deal with his religious friends who had come to help him, only they came in the mind of the flesh. And within this fallen condition, corrupted by the knowledge of good and evil, they sit for seven days until Job finally began to speak, and describe the time of the Great Tribulation. "Let that day be darkness; let not God regard it from above, neither let the light shine upon it."[9] Job begins to describe the prophecies regarding the tribulation period perfectly. The book of Joel reveals the tribulation.

> *A day of darkness and of gloominess, a day of clouds and of thick darkness, as the morning spread upon the mountains: a great people and a strong; there hath not*

> *been ever the like, neither shall be any more after it, even to the years of many generations. Joel 2:2*

The day of the Lord is a day of darkness and not light. Job continues saying, "Let darkness and the shadow of death stain it; let a cloud dwell upon it; let the blackness of the day terrify it."[10] Does that sound like the Great Tribulation? The prophet Joel writes of the tribulation speaking of the people, "Before their face the people shall be much pained: all faces shall gather blackness."[11]

Job continues saying, "Let the stars of the twilight thereof be dark; let it look for light, but have none; neither let it see the dawning of the day"[12] In the book of Isaiah we also read, "And the stars of heaven and the constellations thereof shall not give their light"[13] Isaiah is speaking about the Day of the Lord. The prophet has just finished talking about the coming of the mighty army of God, the anointed ones who come forth from the Lord, and now Isaiah tells us the stars of heaven will not give their light, for it is a day of only darkness that is coming.

Job continues his description of the Great Tribulation saying, "Why is light given to him that is in misery, and life unto the bitter in soul; who long for death, but it comes not; and dig for it more than for hid treasures; Which rejoice exceedingly, and are glad, when they can find the grave?"[14] At this point Job actually wanted to die, and he wished he had never been born, for the fire got so hot and the pain so intense and the misery so overwhelming, that despite all of God's blessings in the past, now Job desires death, and yet, he says it flees from him.

The people during the Great Tribulation will be looking for death and be unable to find it. The book of Revelation declares:

"And in those days shall men seek death, and shall not find it; and shall desire to die, and death shall flee from them."[15] During the tribulation period, people are going to desire death, but death will flee from them. There is no reason left for living, and the faces will all be painted black. Job has described the Great Tribulation.

Job continues saying, "For my sighing cometh before I eat and my roarings are poured out like the waters."[16] Job groans when he awakens every morning, for the first thing that comes upon him is the misery of his pain and he groans as he awakens in the ashes of his life. Job would awaken every morning in pain and anguish of soul. There was not a day that he awoke with comfort or joy, for every day for Job was full of only darkness and there was no light in them. He was groaning in agony before he even got out of bed. That is what the Great Tribulation is going to be like for the many.

And that is what the trial of fire has been like for the few who have been chosen to stand with the lamb on Mount Zion during the time of fire which comes soon to test all of the hearts of the men who dwell upon the earth. This was not "your best life now" or some fantasy version of the gospel, this was the hard-core reality of the cross working real death in the heart of the most righteous man on the planet, and it cut him to the bone. There was real blood spilled too. He suffered the loss of real lives, and all that he loved burned up in the fires right before his eyes. Then he carried this pain and sorrow in his soul while his body was burning within. This was his taste of the cross. And while Job is in this incredible fire, grieving over the loss of everything in his life, now we get to meet Job's religious friends. They come to him with the best of intentions, but they come within the mind of the flesh, and their judgment is distorted by their knowledge of good and evil. They do not come with the mind of the Spirit of God, nor do they speak the truth to him in love.

Job's friends give him the following religious counsel: first, they accuse Job of his very grief. His friends make the statement, "it touches you and you are troubled?" They actually accuse Job, because he is so broken, and because of the fire he is going through. Then they accuse him of being guilty, saying, "when has the innocent perished?" Then they condemn Job before God, and remind him that he has been forsaken by all of the saints, and has no friends left to help him. Finally, they promise him deliverance, once God has finished judging him for his sin, after he has been corrected. And then the grand finale, when they declare in pride, that their knowledge and judgments are true, because they searched it out in the Scriptures. Their judgment is true, they are right, for surely God is judging Job for some hidden sin, and Job should hear their rebuke for his own good.

Job's friends first rebuke him, reminding him, you are the man who instructed many, you uplifted those that have fallen, you strengthened the feeble knees. Job was a rock of stability and was there to help everyone else, but now they say "it is come upon thee, and thou faintest; it touches thee, and thou art troubled."[17] Notice how his friends minimize what happened to Job; they tell him, "it touched you." Are you kidding me? God destroyed Job. It did not just touch him; it crushed him into the ground. But his friends are chiding Job for the fact that he is broken hearted in in the midst of all of the misery the Lord has brought upon him. They are actually judging Job for his broken heart, as God has brought him to the end of himself, through the total devastation of his life.

Job was experiencing the cross, and the death of his own carnal mind, the version of the cross the Father called him to bear, and it is breaking Job. Job is being broken in this process, and his friends are looking down on him and saying, "why are you troubled." And then, they accuse him of being guilty, saying, "Remember, I pray thee, whoever perished, being innocent? or when were the righteous ever cut off?"[18]

When were the righteous ever cut off? That is the accusation that was brought against him. Whoever perished being innocent? When was a righteous man ever killed or judged? Was there ever a righteous man killed while being innocent? Did God ever condemn a righteous man to death? And that was their religious model. God would never condemn a righteous man, and yet God obviously has condemned you. This was their counsel to Job. Can we think of any righteous man that was ever condemned? I can think of one who I know very well, and his name is Jesus. And he died on account of us, so that his blood would cover our sin.

Job's friends are arguing with him, that his trial could only be occurring because of some hidden sin, for when were the righteous ever condemned? When did God ever take a righteous man and put them through this kind of suffering, to the point that he wished he could have died? But they did not know about the ministry of Jesus, or the fact that God calls each of his saints to carry their own cross. They had a religious model that if God was with you, you would be rich and you would be only blessed. The only way anything bad could happen was if you were wicked and under the curse. But this is the opposite of the way God actually works.

The wicked in this life are under temporary mercy, while one day, they will face eternal judgment. The righteous are under temporary judgment and they will receive eternal mercy. As God chastises and corrects and purges his saints, he brings the rod of judgment, but the judgment is only temporary, for unto them is reserved eternal mercy. But the religious model of that day, which is much like ours, is the individuals that have been through great affliction are somehow worth less than the good people in church who have never really seen the furnace of affliction up close and personal in their lives.

His friends also accuse him of having been abandoned by everyone, arguing that the righteous are never abandoned. Were the righteous ever abandoned? Joseph was abandoned by his brothers, when they sold him into slavery into Egypt. It would be safe to say that Joseph had an abandonment issue in his life. Jesus was abandoned, betrayed and forsaken by all of his disciples. So, it is accurate to say the righteous do get abandoned at times.

Yet they are accusing Job saying, "You don't even have any friends left." They came to comfort Job, only now they are offended by his grief. His refusal to accept their condemnation of him has offended their pride, so now they are kicking him when he is down. Then they tell Job, "happy is the man whom God corrects, therefore despise not the chastening of the Almighty." Their words may be doctrinally correct but the Scripture also says, "Weep with those who weep."

Imagine if a friend were to call and tell you the following: he was fired from his job this morning, and when he arrived home, he found the sheriff in his driveway, and they informed him that his wife and children were killed in a car accident on the way home from church. They asked him to come down to the morgue to identify the bodies. When he returned home, he found his house burning down, and then he learned he contracted some terrible disease. His body is now wrecked in pain, and you decide to come over and try to comfort him.

When you arrive, you find he is almost dead from the disease, and then, some friend from church stops by and says, "happy is the man whom God corrects, despise not the chastening of the Lord, you should not be depressed, you should be rejoicing God is correcting you brother." What would you do? I would punch that man in the face. In the midst of that much grief, the Scripture says, "weep with those who weep." You do not quote a hard Bible verse to someone who just had their family killed. Or come in and tell them it is because of some secret sin, and God does not do this to righteous people anyway. But do not worry, when God is done correcting you, you will be fine. You can rejoice in that fact. What an insult. Though doctrinally true, it would have been piercing to his already wounded heart.

"I am just telling you the truth brother." Maybe so, but you are not speaking the truth in love. To someone who just had his life destroyed, you could have found a Scripture that was a little more comforting, instead of being critical and judgmental. This is what comes out of the mind of the flesh, and out of our knowledge of good and evil. This is what we give to each other, when we are not speaking the truth in love, inspired by the

Holy Spirit, but rather are being animated by our pride and speaking out of the dark counsel of our own mind.

Then, they say the most outrageous thing of all, after they sum up all of their rebukes of Job, they say unto him, "Lo, we have searched it, and so it is; hear it, and know thou it for thy good."[19] I am rebuking you, but it is for your own good. I am judging you for your good. I am criticizing and slandering you for your good. I am doing all this through my knowledge of good and evil, but it is for your good, brother. And you should know this, I have read the Bible and I know that I am right! We have all heard this before from people: "I've read the Bible." Oh you did, really? That is great. The ultimate declaration of rebuke is when they tell him, "We have searched it out, and so it is."

Look at the audacity and the pride in these people. "We read it in the Bible and there is no way we missed anything." And yet they missed everything. We will find that out later in the book, when the Lord shows up. From that point, Job begins to talk about how God has become his enemy. Job is now looking at everything in the negative; he has heard the accusation of his friends, and he begins to conclude that the Lord is now against him. And his friends were there speaking for the devil. The evil one is the king over all of the sons of pride, and every word that is spoken in pride actually comes out of the darkness. That may upset some people, but it is the truth, because the spirit of pride is of the spirit of Satan, and he can speak through any one of us if we give him place through the pride in our minds.

Then, in chapter 6, Job begins to speak and says, "Oh that I might have my request and that God would grant me that which I long for." Job has one prayer request left. God please kill me. At this point Job is praying to die. He is going through the cross. He has been forsaken, falsely accused, suffered the loss of all things, and now, even the faith within him is beginning to fail. So, Job seeks the only refuge he believes is left to him; and so he asks the Almighty to end his life.

In chapter 7, Job says, "When I lay in my bed, with dreams he terrifies me in the night." Job cannot even find comfort while asleep. There was no relief for him. The prophet Jeremiah had a similar experience. He shares his own feelings in the book of Lamentations, chapter 3. Jeremiah experienced something very similar to what Job went through. Listen to Jeremiah's words:

> *I am the man who has seen the furnace of affliction by the rod of his wrath. He led me into darkness, and not light. Against me his hand is turned all the day. He broke my bones, he surrounded me with gall and travail. He set me in dark places, as if I was dead. He hedged me about and I cannot cry out. He made my chain heavy, and when I cry he shuts out my prayer. My paths are made crooked, he turns aside all my ways, he broke me in pieces. He made me desolate. He bent his bow and set me is the mark for his arrow. I was a derision to all my people and their song all the day. He filled me with bitterness and he broke my teeth with gravel. He covered me with ashes, he removed my soul from peace, I have forgotten my prosperity, I said my strength and my hope has perished from the Lord. I have no hope left. Remembering my afflictions, the wormwood and the gall, my soul has them still in remembrance, and is humbled within me. Therefore I recall to my mind and I have hope, it is of the Lord's mercy that we are not utterly consumed. Because his compassions fail not, for they are new every morning. Great is his faithfulness, for the Lord is my portion. Therefore I will hope in him.*

What Job went through, Jeremiah went through as well. Go read Lamentations chapter 3 for yourselves. Everything that Job experienced, Jeremiah also got a full cup. This is the cup of trembling, and it is reserved for God's most precious saints. Notice what it produced, for Jeremiah said, "I remember and therefore I am humbled within."

When you have been through this process, your pride does not survive. It is amazing, but it does not survive. You get utterly emptied out. Hallelujah! Do not take my word for it, look at the Scriptures. In chapter 19, Job tells us, "my friends have forsaken me, and those that I love have turned against me." A part of this furnace of affliction and the cross experience, includes having his few remaining friends come and kick sand in his face. They rebuked him in their pride, and tore him up verbally. All of his other friends detested him. They actually loathed him, so Job had no comforters at all.

Then in chapter 38, the Lord finally responds to Job and confronts him, for previously, in the discourse with his friends, Job had made the statement, "Oh that I could talk to the Most High, and tell him of my complaint." Job had wanted to talk to God, because what was happening to him did not seem fair. Job had a complaint, and he wanted to tell the Lord a thing or two. He thought, I am going to talk to the Lord about this, and he is going to hear from me. Oh really? I guess we are not done in the furnace! Because by the time God is done, we are not going to be thinking or talking like that anymore. Then, the Lord shows up, and he rebukes Job for his words that were without knowledge. The words which brought the Lord's rebuke are discussed in detail in the Dark Counsel chapter of *Search the Scriptures: Out of the Darkness*.

> *Then the LORD answered Job out of the whirlwind, and said, who is this that darkens counsel by words without knowledge? Gird up now thy loins like a man; for I will demand of thee, and answer thou me. Where were thou when I laid the foundations of the earth? declare, if thou hast understanding. Joel 38:1-4*

Job answers the Lord, "I know you can do everything, and I am not going to hide knowledge by words of dark counsel anymore." This was God's main rebuke, not only of Job, but also his friends, for they were bringing only dark counsel through their words which were utterly without knowledge. The entire religious model of the carnal mind of man is false, and full of dark counsel which only comes from this present fallen age. Like Job's friends, we have so many doctrines in our minds that have a foundation based on dark counsel, and yet, we are so convinced we are right, because we read the book. We searched it out, and we "*know*" that it is so. "I am about to disappear in the pre-tribulation rapture, and I am certain of it." But why then are we all still sitting here?

We too are so convinced, and so full of ourselves, which is why God must empty us out as well. Job says, "I uttered things that I understood not." People ask questions and they do not even understand the question they have asked. Job goes on to say, "I've heard of you, by the hearing of the ear, but now my eyes see you and therefore I abhor myself, and I repent in dust and ashes." The attitude in Job is no longer, I cannot wait to talk to the Lord. He believed he had a valid complaint with the Lord. Why is a just man being destroyed? And then when Job finally does see the Lord, he says, "I abhor myself."

The Scripture says in the last days, many will become offended and betray one another, and hate one another. There is a spirit of offense at work, and I caution you, be on the lookout, because it is going to try to divide every family, every relationship, and holy assembly. For the spirit of offense will try to come in, and it is going to become easy for you to get offended, if you still have pride. And if you do, the enemy still has a button in you to push. But once you have been offended with yourself, you do not get as easily offended with other people. Job saw himself for who he really was, in the light of God's truth, and he became offended with himself.

Job thought he was innocent, and he wondered, why has God become my enemy? I did not do anything to deserve this, and it is not fair. In his own mind, he had a case, but once he steps into the light of God's holiness, Job suddenly says, "I loathe myself." No longer is he justified in his own eyes. No longer does he have any ground at all to stand on before the Lord. He repents in dust and ashes saying, "God, I did not know I had pride in me. Who am I to think I can stand in your presence and bring any charge before you? Who am I to even question you? Who am I to even think of bringing a complaint against the Almighty?"

And that is the end of Job. There came a day that God brought Job to the end of himself, and to the revelation of Jesus Christ. God had revealed himself to Job, and he saw the Lord in all of his holiness, and then he saw himself for what he truly was. Job, the most righteous man on the earth, who had just been through the most intense purging process any man would ever see, short of the cross itself, who thought he had a case, and a complaint before the Lord, suddenly is utterly emptied of himself, and all he can say is, "I am offended with me." God is going to do this same work in every one of us; it is only a question of when.

In the 144,000, he is doing this right now. For most of the church, this is going to happen when they reach the judgment seat of Christ, which is the bema seat in the heavens. You are going to see the Lord, and come forward when he calls your name and then it is going to be your turn. He is going to open your eyes, and you are going to see for the first time in your life, everything you did and said for what it really was in the light of God's holiness. I guarantee you, this day is coming for all of us, because the Lord talked to me about this. You will either undergo this process now, or you will do it later, but eventually everyone must go through this. We will all repent totally, either now or later. You can do it now, in the privacy of your own heart between just you and the Lord, or if you are too afraid, or you want to keep sinning a while longer, or for whatever reason, you are not yet ready to completely repent, the furnace of affliction awaits you. But, if you do not want to go there, you can always choose to wait and, if you are really his, then you will deal with some of this in the very presence of the Lord. But it is not going to be any easier to deal with it then. There is going to be a lot of weeping at the bema seat. But the Lord is going to wipe away every tear, and take all of those sins and put them in the sea of forgetfulness. The next day in heaven, it will be like it never happened. So, for all of us, God has a new beginning.

> *Bread corn is bruised; because he will not always be threshing it, nor break it with the wheel of his cart, nor bruise it with his horsemen. This also cometh forth from the LORD of hosts, which is wonderful in counsel, and excellent in working. Isaiah 28:28-29*

The bread corn is *bruised,* and the word is דקק, *daw-kak* and it means; to crush, to break into pieces, to turn into dust, to be made very small, and to be stamped into the ground. To be hammered. That is a good picture of what happened to Job. The corn is crushed, but he will not always be threshing it. Nor will God bruise it with the four horsemen that are coming, who are about to ride across this planet as the book of Revelation opens.

The bread corn is a picture of the anointed remnant, which are crushed. But the Lord will not always be threshing it, and that word for *always* is נצח, *netsach* and it means; the goal, the bright object in the distance that we are traveling towards, of glory and splendor. It also means truthfulness, strength and victory. He is not going to always be threshing it.

So, the process that Job went through, and that we all go through, does not last forever. And the corn, which is the anointed remnant of the feast of First Fruit, is destined to become as the handful of corn presented before the Lord in the Temple that is pictured in Scripture as lifted up on the top of the mountains. This is a picture of the 144,000, presented as a vessel for the use of the Lord. They are the *yeledeem,* the "man-child" company whom the Lord has given to Israel. They are bruised, and they go through the cross, and through the fire, but they do not have the four Horsemen of the book of Revelation trampling them under, because they are already done. The work in them has been completed, and on the day the Great Tribulation begins, you will see the Son of Man revealed within them.

> *There shall be an handful of corn in the earth upon the top of the mountains; the fruit thereof shall shake like Lebanon:*

and they of the city shall flourish like grass of the earth.
Psalm 72:16

There is a handful of corn in the hand of the Lord, and they are his portion. They are the first fruit that Father God has given. They are going to be used by the King to complete the ministry of Jesus Christ. And how clean do these vessels need to be? Thoroughly clean! So, how hot must the furnace be - hotter than you could ever imagine.

God is going to purify us, and we have a choice in how it gets done, though we do not have a choice on whether or not it is going to happen. God never asks our permission for anything. He tells us what he is going to do. He told me, "you can either come willingly or I will take your life by force" and he told me "you haven't seen anything yet." These fires can get so hot, dear saints, trust me in this, it can get hotter than you could even believe is possible. It is beyond your comprehension. But, when you are in that furnace of affliction and the time of tribulation, which is coming upon all of us quite soon, you will stop worrying about the things that seemed so important to you when you were in the mind of the flesh, and start thanking God that you are not going to hell for eternity. Think about it, we were chosen in a furnace of affliction, but then we are all going to paradise. What are we complaining about? As Paul said, this light affliction is not worthy to be compared to the glory that is about to be revealed through us. Okay maybe it is not such a light affliction for some of us, but it is still not worthy to be compared to the glory which shall be revealed within us.

"Behold, I have refined thee, but not with silver; I have chosen thee in the furnace of affliction"[20] and the word for *affliction* is, עֳנִי, *on-ee'* and it means; depression, misery and trouble. In the book of Genesis, Joseph said, "God has caused me to be fruitful in the land of my affliction." Jeremiah, as we read in Lamentations, also said, "I am the man who has seen affliction." Isaiah's prophecy reveals that the Lord also shared in our afflictions saying, "In all their afflictions, he was afflicted."[21]

Jesus, speaking in the gospel of Mark said, "for in those days there shall be affliction, such as never was from the beginning of creation from which God created until this time, and neither shall there be again."[22] The word for *affliction* in this text is θλιὶψις, *thlip'-sis,* which means pressure, anguish, to be burdened and persecuted, to go to through tribulation and trouble.

Moses also warned the children of Israel in the prophecy of Deuteronomy where he said, "when you're in tribulation and all these things come upon you, even in the last days, if you turn to the Lord your God, and shall be obedient to his voice, for the Lord your God is a merciful God, he will not forsake you neither will you destroy you nor forget the covenant of your fathers and that which he swore unto them."[23]

Jesus spoke to his disciples of this hour, and his word speaks to each of us today, in this time, the time when these words will be fulfilled:

> *A woman when she is in travail has sorrow, because her hour is come: but as soon as she is delivered of the child, she remembers no more the anguish, for joy that a man is born into the world. Do you now believe? Behold, the hour comes, yea, it now comes, and you shall all be scattered, every man to his own, and shall leave me alone: and yet I am not alone, because the Father is with me. These things I*

have spoken unto you, that in me you might have peace. In the world you shall have tribulation: but be of good cheer; I have overcome the world. John 16:21, 31-33

That Woman Jezebel

Beloved, believe not every spirit, but try the spirits whether they be of God: because many false prophets have come. 1 John 4:1

Now the Spirit speak expressly, in the latter days some shall depart from the faith, giving heed to seducing spirits, and doctrines of devils; and speaking lies in hypocrisy. 1Timothy 4:1-2

The enemy of our souls comes to make war on the saints; and in these last days, the level of warfare and resistance is only going to increase. The spirits of wickedness in high places fight against the people of God, but at the same time, the Lord is calling his people to overcome. Where sin abounds, grace abounds more. The day that we are now entering into is not the day of muttering and peeping spirits in the dark, rather it is the Day of the Lord, in which the Lord is going to rule and reign through the power of his light and truth in righteousness from above.

Darkness is going to cover the earth, and a deep darkness is coming upon the minds of the people, but the light of revelation and truth along with the power of God is coming upon his people. God is calling us to a higher place, and to come into the inner court within the temple in the Spirit; and this is not a cliché, but a spiritual reality, and it is the truth.

I have never believed in cliché Christianity. This is one of the main attributes of the Charasmatic church, which has been deceived and where the faith embraced by many, is only in words which have no basis in reality at all. The Spirit of God is calling the church to come back to the truth, and back to their first love. We must have a higher level of commitment to the Lord, if we want to overcome what is coming. This requires a higher level of repentance, a deeper searching of the heart, and a greater commitment to the Lord. We all must put off those things which hinder us, laying down our lives and crucifying our flesh.

For those who desire to enter in to the place of true sanctification, it also requires fasting and prayer. In this hour, the remnant is being called into seasons of fasting and prayer, and into times of long-term fasting. The Daniel fast is a long-term fast and in the time of fasting and prayer, and of turning our hearts back to the Lord, returning to our first love, and returning to the place of total commitment to Jesus, we are called to leave behind the mixed multitude that wants to hide their sin and continue in their compromise. But only a remnant is going to survive and endure the Day of the Lord, and they are not going to be found in the outer court of compromise. They also not have a silver wedge hidden in their tents like Achan did; rather they are being called to a total commitment of their hearts in order to actually enter the land of promise.

In the days ahead, the abyss is going to open, and demonic entities are going to come forth and transition into this realm. Then all of the children of darkness, will become possessed of this darkness, and do their will. We are going to have to stand against the Dragon, and against these forces of darkness. This will require a level of holiness and sanctification that, quite candidly, most of us have never known. But that is why God is opening our eyes, and why he has provided time for us to get ready. Judgment begins in the house of God, and the wake-up call has come to the house of God. The choices that are given to humanity are first given to the house of God. For the people who call themselves Christian are now being led by the Lord into the valley of decision.

Multitudes of professing Christians, who claim to be spirit filled, are going to be taken into the valley of decision where they will choose which God they will serve, and there we will discover, who the true God in Israel is. Is the Lord Jehovah still God? Or has Ba'al become the Lord? Choose wisely in that valley. The Lord is going to equip you with skills, and he is going to give you knowledge and wisdom, so that you would have understanding, so you do not get deceived, because you cannot follow the false guides any longer, and you do not want the counsel from muttering spirits. You must not receive any guidance from the spirits of divination; you must learn to look to the Lord and to him only.

The Lord wants to break off of you, the yokes of the enemy. We must learn to cut off all of the cords and the snares of the Fowler as well. You are going to learn how to cut those out of your life so that you are no longer victimized by an enemy that has come in and operates unseen among us. He has been looting and pillaging within the church for years. The Scriptures present for us a picture of this hour in Psalm 74:

> *O God, why hast thou cast us off forever? Why does your anger smoke against the sheep of thy pasture? Remember thy congregation, which thou hast purchased of old; the*

rod of thine inheritance, which thou hast redeemed; this mount Zion, wherein thou hast dwelt. Lift up thy feet unto the perpetual desolations; even all that the enemy hath done wickedly in the sanctuary. Thy enemies roar in the midst of thy congregations; they set up their ensigns for signs. Psalm 74:1-4

This is a picture of the desolation of the charismatic churches at the time of the end. Churches which were at one time spirit filled only now are full of spirits that need to be cast out. Look what has come upon the congregations which at one time were walking in victory, full of the Holy Spirit. Over the last thirty years, the charismatic movement has been destroyed. It has become a desolation, exactly as described in Psalm 74. For this Scripture is a picture of what has come upon the church in America.

The enemy now roars in the midst of your congregations. The false prophets lift up their voices, the diviners and the necromancers prophesy, and the spirit of Jezebel runs rampant. And her slaves, which she calls her sons, create more and more confusion every day; and when the people of God, come to church looking for hope and for relief, they return home more bound than when they first walked through the door.

They have cast fire into thy sanctuary, they have defiled by casting down the dwelling place of thy name to the ground. They said in their hearts, Let us destroy them together: they have burned up all the synagogues of God in the land. We see not our signs: there is no more any prophet: neither is there among us any that knows how long. Psalm 74:7-8

THE ENEMY HAS CAST FIRE INTO THE CHURCHES

The enemy has cast fire into the churches, and has defiled the people of God by casting them down. Many people are falling under the false anointing which has come, while the first love of many has grown cold. All the while, they are being slain in the spirit, and most of this is just a counterfeit. They have cast down the dwelling place of God's name to the ground. The dwelling place of God's name is his people, and they have been literally casting them down to the ground. The Scriptures reveal that only God's enemies fall backwards, while his friends always fall forward on their faces before him.

> *Jesus therefore, knowing all things that should come upon him, went forth, and said unto them, 'Who seek ye?' They answered him, 'Jesus of Nazareth.' Jesus saith unto them, 'I am.' And Judas also, which betrayed him, stood with them. As soon then as he had said unto them, 'I am', they went backward, and fell to the ground. John 18:4-6*

When God first made his covenant with Abraham, the Great Patriarch fell on his face before the Lord.[24] The Scripture records how Moses, Joshua, Ezekiel and Daniel, all fell on their faces before the Lord.[25] The disciples fell on their faces when they heard the voice of the Father on the Mount of Transfiguration.[26] Jesus himself fell on his face before God in the garden of Gethsemane. "Then he said unto them, My soul is exceeding sorrowful, even unto death: tarry ye here, and watch with me. And he went a little further, and fell on his face, and prayed."[27]

Whereas the enemies of God, and those upon whom the curses have come, always fall backward. "Dan shall be a serpent by the way, an adder in the path, that bites the horse heels, so that his rider shall fall backward."[28] Isaiah prophesied of a people who would be rejected of the Lord, and as such, they would go and fall backwards, and then be broken, snared and taken. "But the word of the LORD was unto them precept upon precept, precept upon precept; line upon line, line upon line; here a little, and there a little; that they might go, and *fall backward*, and be broken, and snared, and taken."[29]

THEY CAME IN AMONG US

They said in their hearts, "Let us destroy them." And so, the people with no discernment and no understanding have all fallen backwards. Now they have been broken, snared, and some have been taken, and those who are taken will not be coming back.

This was a conspiracy from hell itself, and it involved the entire satanic church. The witches and warlocks were actively engaged in this attack on the church. They organized together and then they came among us to destroy us. And we neither perceived nor understood it; so therefore, they prospered in their evil work. I have attended charismatic churches where I met witches who revealed themselves as such, who later went forward during the ministry time and prayed for and laid hands upon the unsuspecting people. I sat in the church and watched this satanic invasion firsthand. I witnessed it with my own eyes, when the false worship first came in, and the demons filled the sanctuary with darkness.

So, they came in among us. They joined our prayer groups, and they were part of the ministry teams. Some of them came as pastors, and teachers; and some of them came as prophets and so they overran the churches. They began to dominate from the shadows; they brought in the false worship which opened the door for all the devils. Then they introduced the false prophets who brought with them the doctrines of demons. Then when the Lord became so grieved, that the Holy Spirit left, a flood of filth from hell came in the form of a false anointing, and then everything went off the rails entirely.

TAKEN CAPTIVE TO BABYLON

That is the true condition of most charismatic churches today. There is a remnant that is still seeking the Lord, but most of the people have been carried away into captivity. They were taken into captivity in the spirit, to Babylon. What happened to Israel in the natural has happened to the church in the spirit. Just as ancient Israel was taken into slavery in Babylon for turning from the Lord, so too the American churches who have forsaken the Lord, have been carried off into slavery in Babylon, only they were taken as slaves by the lying spirits.

The enemy has burned down the churches of God in the spirit, and so the people cannot see their signs anymore nor are there any true prophets among them. There is nothing real about most of the prophetic words found within the charismatic church today, nor is there any among them who know how long. How many of these so called prophets warned about the events of 9/11? How many have seen what is now coming upon the land? There is only a remnant, who are true prophets, and there is only a small company of men of wisdom can give true insight into this time, and what is about to come upon the land, but for the most part, in the churches of America, you can tag it and bag it, because they are done.

LORD HOW LONG WILL THE ENEMY REPROACH

The Scripture cries out, "Lord, how long will the enemy reproach and blaspheme thy name in the church?" But the Lord is going to have the victory. Psalm 74 declares, "You broke the heads of leviathan in pieces, and gave him to be meat to the people inhabiting the wilderness."[30] The victory will be given to those who have fled from these abominations, and who now inhabit the wilderness.

In the wilderness, the word of the Lord will come forth again, even as it did 2,000 years ago. John the Baptist came in the spirit and the power of Elijah, and before the face of the Lord. The Scripture testifies of him: "And the child grew, and waxed strong in the spirit, and was in the deserts till the day of his showing unto Israel." [31] The word for *desert* is *eremos*[32] which means; to be lonesome, living in a wasteland; to dwell in the desert, in a desolate and solitary place, in the wilderness.

John was prepared by God in the wilderness, and it was there that he received the word of the Lord. It was on the backside of the desert, in the wilderness, that Moses led his flock; it was there that he came upon the mountain of God, even to Horeb. There, "the Lord appeared unto him in a flame of fire out of the midst of a bush."[33] It is in the wilderness that the Lord also promised to do a new thing, and to "make a way in the wilderness, and rivers in the desert."[34]

God called his people out of Egypt, and sent Moses unto Pharaoh saying: "The LORD God of the Hebrews hath sent me unto thee, saying, let my people go, that they may serve me in the wilderness."[35]

He is speaking the same words today to the king of Egypt in the spirit, who is the ruler over all of this darkness in the church. The Lord is calling his people to come out of Egypt spiritually today, and to leave Babylon. King David hid from Saul in the wilderness, waiting for the Lord to establish his throne. The Proverbs declare, "It is better to dwell in the wilderness, than in a house full of contentious people."[36] Today, much of the church is filled with people of whom the Lord said, "Bring only an offering of strife and contention in my house."

The Song of Solomon contains a prophecy of the remnant in this hour: "Who is this that cometh up from the wilderness, leaning upon her beloved?"[37] For the remnant and the men of wisdom appointed in this hour, all come forth from out of the wilderness, for it is there, that the true word of God is still found.

THE DAY IS THINE

The Psalm goes on to declare: "The day is thine, the night also is thine: thou hast prepared the light and the sun."[38] Which day is the Lord's Day? The day which is the Lord's Day is called *The Day of the Lord*. "Remember this, that the enemy hath reproached, O LORD, and that the foolish people have blasphemed thy name."[39] Psalm 74 is a prophecy regarding the church, and not unbelievers. This prophecy is about the foolish people within the church who are blaspheming the name of the Lord. That is how terrible the true condition of the church is in this hour. In this chapter, I am going to reveal how this is occurring and how you can identify it. Because you do not want to be anywhere around those people and you do not want them speaking into your life. You do not want to hear their declarations of darkness and you do not want to listen to that divination spirit when it rises up. You want to separate yourself from all of these abominations, as much as is possible, and seek the Lord only, because this is the time of separation, and God is coming to separate the wheat from the chaff and the true from the false.

> *Deliver not the soul of thy turtledove unto the multitude of the wicked: forget not the congregation of thy poor forever. Psalm 74:19*

The soul of the turtledove is a picture of the innocent saint who still loves the Lord and is therefore precious in God's eyes. The psalmist is crying to the Lord, and praying that the innocent saints would not be turned over to the multitude of the wicked that are now "the church." Instead of a congregation of the righteous, much of the church has now become the congregation of the damned, and it is full of the multitudes of people who are perishing. They have big numbers, for "*many*" walk with them down the wide road to perdition.

THE DARK PLACES OF THE EARTH

> *Have respect unto your covenant oh Lord: for the dark places of the earth are full of the habitations of cruelty. Psalm 74:20*

Wherever you find the darkness, you will find the spirit of cruelty and that is one of the ways you will know what you are dealing with. When these false spirits that have come among us are challenged or uncovered, they turn vicious on you. Love your enemies; forget about it, it will never happen in Satan's camp. You will know them by their fruit and their words will always betray them. This is the terrible time that would come at the end of the age; these are the perilous times which the Scripture warned us would come in the very end of the last days. In the book of Revelation, Jesus uncovers the spirit of the false prophet, which had come within the church.

> *"I have a few things against thee, because you suffer that woman Jezebel, which calls herself a prophetess, to teach and to seduce my servants to commit fornication, and to eat things sacrificed unto idols."* Revelation 2:20

"That woman Jezebel" and Jesus refers to her as, "that woman." The Lord has revealed a number of insights into how the spirit of antichrist has been operating in our midst, disguising himself as a minister of light. The Lord is going to deal with that woman Jezebel, and with all her sons of darkness, for the hour has come for them to be discovered for who they really are, and for them to be revealed to the people who still love the truth:

> *For God is my King of old, working salvation in the midst of the earth. O let not the oppressed return ashamed: let the poor and needy praise thy name. Arise, O God, plead thine own cause: remember how the foolish man reproaches thee daily. Forget not the voice of thine enemies: the tumult of those that rise up against thee increases continually.* Psalm 74:12, 22-23

For the voice of the enemy has increased continually within the congregation of the saints, but the Lord is going to put to shame all of the sons of darkness, and deliver his children who have been oppressed by them, silencing them once and for all.

BELIEVE NOT EVERY SPIRIT

Beloved, do not believe every spirit, but try the spirits whether they are of God: because ***many*** *false prophets have gone forth into the world."*[40] *"Now the Spirit expressly speaks, and expressly warns us, that in the last days there will be those who will depart from the true faith, and they will give heed to seducing spirits, and doctrines of devils; and they will be speaking lies fashioned in hypocrisy; emanating from consciences seared as with a burning iron. I Timothy 4:1-2*

Seducing spirits were prophesied to come within the church, and we were warned that there would be some who would give heed to them. The word *seducing* is πλάνος, *planos* and it means; a roving spirit, or a tramp; a homeless demon which is an impostor. It comes only to mislead, and to deceive and seduce the church. How is it possible that the church could follow an impostor? Because these seducing spirits have come masquerading as the Holy Spirit. The seducing spirits masquerade as spirits of light, and when they fall on the people, the people sense the power of a spirit coming upon them, but it is not the Lord. The people have all fallen from the truth within the apostate church, and they have turned back from obeying the Lord. They have decided to go back and walk in the ways of compromise, so they can no longer discern the difference. After the Lord removed his presence from among them, the people came and gathered together and they still wanted an anointing, to experience the feeling of a spirit coming upon them. So, the seducing spirits came and did exactly that. And now the people began to feel another spirit coming upon them, only they could not discern the difference. This is astonishing, but it is also true.

A FALSE ANOINTING

It is within this false anointing, that the false prophets minister their words of lies. This is a Kundalini anointing, which comes right out of hell, and if you do not believe me, or if you want to see this for yourself, then open up a YouTube page on your computer and search for the program entitled, "World Revival Church satanic warning."[41] In part two of this video message, you will see this demonic anointing pick up a pastor and throw him through the air. It looks as if he is being devoured by a shark in the spirit world. It is horrible to watch, but if you do not understand what I am talking about, that there is a counterfeit out there, go and see it for yourself.

So these seducing spirits have come in speaking lies. That word for *lies* is ψευδολόγος, *pseudologos* and it means erroneous Christian doctrine. These lying spirits and the deceivers through which they speak are introducing heresy, for these lies are spoken in hypocrisy, from a feigned heart which itself is deceived. The word for *hypocrisy* is ὑπόκρισις, *hupokrisis* and it means; acting under a feigned heart, to be deceitful and to bring condemnation and hypocrisy. They are twisting the Scriptures while they are lying for the purposes of gaining an advantage over the people, for the money, or for the control it gives them, and to lift themselves up. These people are not only lying to you, they are lying to themselves as well.

AS YOU THINK IN YOUR HEART

As a man thinks in his heart so is he. Proverbs 23:7

As you think in your heart. The essence of who we are, and the essence of what spirit we are of, lies within our thought life. That is why the Scripture commands us to "take our thoughts captive." You cannot remain in the anointing if your thought life goes back to the ways of the flesh. The anointing will leak right out of you, and you will utterly quench it. You cannot walk in the Holy Spirit, if your thought life is filled with lies and deception, and the strong delusion that came from the seducing spirits. You cannot walk in the truth and the lie at the same time; for a little bit of leaven, will leaven the whole lump.

The world that we perceive, and our very identity, our consciousness of our self, is ultimately understood through the words that we choose; the words we meditate on in our hearts, the words we believe in our minds, and the words that we choose to speak with our mouth.

The words that we have received, and the words that we have declared, impact our lives, but most important are the words that we have chosen to believe. Our worldview and the words, with which we define it, are reinforced by the messages we repeat to ourselves. We speak them, again and again, in our self-talk within our hearts; we meditate upon them in the quiet corridors of our mind, and then we speak them with our tongue. Words are powerful things, for the very power of life and death lies within the words we speak. These words are very important, for their power and their influence affect not only our life, but everyone who hears us. The Lord warned us expressly, that you will give an account for every idle word you speak. And the Lord is not nitpicking, for the words we speak have more power than we realize.

THE WORDS WE RECEIVE

The essence of who we are lies within our thought life. The world we perceive and the very identity of our self is understood through the words we have received, and especially the ones we choose to believe. Our world view is understood through the thoughts we hold in our hearts, and our thoughts are reinforced by the words we tell ourselves. Words are powerful things; the very power of life and death is contained within the words we speak. The words we utter are so important, and so powerful in their impact on us and on everyone around us, that the Lord warns us, we will give an account for every single word we speak.

There are many types of words of to choose within the gallery of man: you can speak words of knowledge, and words of truth, or words without knowledge that darken the truth. There are the words of the wise and the words of a fool. Words that may be proved true and words that will be proved a lie. It will be done unto you according to your words, whether they are godly words or vanity's words. The words that are laid up in your heart create a storehouse within, and the words of the enemy will all fall to the ground in the end. The words of wrath and the words of raging fools, which are found within the words of the multitudes, and shall these words ever end. Righteous words oppose the words that defile; devouring words, slandering words and condemning words are found in the mouths of men who are lost in the vain habitations of darkness.

Words of flattery are mixed with words of deceit, along with lying words, which are words from devils. The words of a true prophet are pure words, pleasant words, and words of praise, filled with faith, hope and love. The word of the Lord alone shall endure to the end, while every other word shall surely fall to the ground. They will either die on their own, or they will produce death within those who erroneously received them. "For by thy words you shall be justified, or by thy words, you shall be condemned."

It is by our words that we enter in; the words we speak, the words we believe, and the words we receive. In this chapter, we are going to look at how the enemy has infiltrated the congregation in order to speak words that were intended to destroy the church. And for the most part they have been very effective, but we are going to uncover them, and give you some tools of discernment, so that you can uproot these lying words out of your life. And then replace these words of desolation and destruction, with words of life, healing and salvation.

First let us look to the word of the Lord, which are the Scriptures of Truth. We should all know and understand that the Scriptures are the Word of God. They are infallible, for they were inspired by the Holy Spirit of Almighty God. The Lord has brought forth his word, as a light in this darkened world, and you must understand that the Word of God is the truth, and it is perfect in every way, and perfect in every day. And if you want to fully comprehend the entire revelations from the Scriptures, then you need to study the original Hebrew and Greek manuscripts using your concordance. And then you should prayerfully seek God's revelation from the reading of his word.

The Scriptures are the word of God and we should know and understand this truth and be certain of it.

There is another word out there, a word that comes through an inspired man, and there is a message from God that comes to us in dreams and visions, and there is wisdom and knowledge from God which comes to us through our intuition. This is the part of our mind where we hear the Lord speaking to us in words that emanate from within our spirit; but most of us cannot hear his voice in our conscious mind as he speaks to our spirit man. The reason we are unaware that it is the Lord speaking to us, is our carnal mind is alienated from our spirit man. We have not yet crucified the mind of the flesh, so the carnal mind is still on his throne, ruling and reigning within many.

THE MIND OF THE FLESH

The carnal mind is on a vacation, a Chevy Chase type of vacation, where it goes off and does whatever seems right in its own eyes. When we are walking in the mind of the flesh, we do not hear the voice of the spirit of God. The Lord speaks through the voice of His spirit, so the things the Lord says to us in the spirit come into our conscious mind through what we perceive as intuition. But the enemy can speak in the same way to us, which is why we have to test all things. Who said that? Did it come from the heart of man, from within our own soul, or was that another one of the voices, the many voices Jesus warned us would come. Or was that word from the Lord?

If you get really close to the Lord, and learn the skill of listening, you will be able to tell the difference between them; between your thoughts, and the enemy. And you will begin to discern, when the things in your intuition have come forth from the spirit of God.

The Lord speaks to each of his children, for the Scriptures declare, "My sheep hear my voice", but the Lord usually speaks to us, first and foremost, through the Word of God, which is the Bible. There is also a gift of prophesy and word of knowledge in the church, and there are people who come among us with a prophetic word, and sometimes they come with a true prophetic word. There are a few who are true prophets in the land, but we were also warned at the time of the end, many false prophets would also come. One of the things that you should know about a true prophet, is you do not have to tell them anything. They speak through the spirit of Almighty God and he knows everything already. You do not have to prep them. They do not need to know what is going on with you, in order to prophesy to you, or in order to make a declaration to you. They can walk up to you on the street, and speak concretely and specifically to you, but not so with the many false prophets. Most of them are putting their hooks in what they know about you.

CONFIRMED BY TWO OR MORE WITNESSES

The most important thing for you to remember about true prophets, is the word they bring you will always be confirmed, both by the word of God, the Bible, and by the Spirit of the Lord. Another true witness about true prophecy, the day will always declare a word came from God. When I have asked the Lord to send a prophet, I do not go looking for them, they come to me, and they come uninvited and on their own. They have come walking up in a restaurant, right up to my table and said to me, "When are you going to begin to teach my people. The

Lord says, 'I have called you teach the people, and I want to begin to teach.'" Reality has vindicated that the Lord has called me to teach the word of God to his people, which is what I am doing in this book.

The Lord will bring his word to you. This whole model of running around seeking to hear words from these people that claim that they have the gift of prophecy is not of the Lord. Jesus warned us that in the last days many false prophets would come. Nowhere in the word of God were we ever told that there would be a true prophetic movement in this final hour. Rather, we were warned, a large number of false prophets would come.

There are two witnesses coming, at the very time of the end, and they will prophesy unto the nations for 42 months, but they are not going to be giving you any personal words of prophecy. They are going to be declaring the judgment of Almighty God upon the wicked and upon Mystery Babylon. They will be speaking prophetically to the entire Earth, and they are going to be declaring the judgments of Almighty God during the Great tribulation and they are going to prophesy the truth. And when they speak, the day shall declare their words were true.

> *And the LORD came down in the pillar of the cloud, and stood in the door of the tabernacle, and called Aaron and Miriam: and they both came forth. And he said, Hear now my words: If there be a prophet among you, I the LORD will make myself known unto him in a vision, and will speak unto him in a dream. My servant Moses is not so, who is faithful in all mine house. With him will I speak mouth to mouth, even apparently, and not in dark speeches; and the similitude of the LORD shall he behold:*

wherefore then were ye not afraid to speak against my servant Moses? And the anger of the LORD was kindled against them. Numbers 12:5-9

MANY FALSE PROPHETS WILL COME

This is the hour Jesus warned us of, when many false prophets would come among us. The Scriptures also warn us that there would be seducing spirits, along with a strong delusion, which would come down upon the people, and then a great falling away would occur within the church. People would become lovers of their own self. The last generation would become a people who were narcissistic, and doctrines of devils would replace the truth in much of the church. A picture of this is in the book of Amos.

> *Behold, the days come, says the Lord GOD, that I will send a famine in the land, not a famine of bread, nor a thirst for water, but of hearing the true word of the LORD: And they shall wander from sea to sea, and from the north even to the east, they shall run to and fro seeking to hear a word from the LORD, and they shall not find it. In that day shall the fair virgins and young men faint for thirst. They that swear by the sin of Samaria, and say, Thy god, O Dan, lives; and, The manner of Beersheba lives; even they shall fall, and never rise up again. Amos 8:11-14*

A FAMINE IN THE LAND OF THE TRUE WORD OF GOD

And they shall not find it. There is a reason why God has called forth a famine in the land, not of bread or water, but of his word. Now we still have our Bibles, and that is the word of

God, so they have not taken the Bible from you yet, but as far as finding the word of God in this hour from some prophet who is wandering around, giving out personal prophetic words, that is very rare in this time. I can count the number of true prophets that I have met over the course of my lifetime on one hand. And then there are the many false prophets who are operating in the counterfeit; they are either pretending and speaking out of their own souls, which is destructive, doing so out of their own deceit or they have a spirit of divination, where the devil is actually bringing forth the prophetic words. And the spirit of divination is very smart; it is smarter than all of us. These are very cunning intelligences, and they know how to make it look real. They also know how to conceal their evil. The thief comes to steal, kill and destroy, and that is their only agenda. For a lying spirit of divination to steal from you, or to kill you or to destroy your life, they first have to get you to buy their lie.

The days of famine in the land have come, a famine for the true word of God. Yet the Lord says you will find me when you seek me with your whole heart. But that takes a lot of effort, and if you are far from the Lord, and you are not hearing the Lord right now, you need to fast and pray, and get serious about seeking the Lord. You need to seek him with all of your heart, all of your strength and with all your effort. He says, "When you seek me with all your heart, you will find me" and when you find him, he will speak to you. But this is the generation of people who are not seeking him with their whole heart, for their hearts are still divided, and they still want to hold onto some of their sin, and keep some of the pleasures of the flesh. They are happy to be a Christian and they love Jesus, they just do not want to go to the cross. Can we just skip that part? For whatever reason, there are scores of people today who are not hearing from the Lord. So what are they doing? Are they humbling themselves, beginning to fast and pray, shutting themselves in with God, and turning off the television and turning away from the pleasures of Babylon and seeking the Lord with all their might? No, that takes too much work; they would rather just get in their car and drive around and go hear the latest man who has coming to town supposedly with the word of God. They would rather call sister Suzy, who has a prophetic word, or they would rather go call on that woman Jezebel and they would rather listen to her slaves whom she calls her sons, who are the prophets of *Ba'al*. We are going to find out that her sons, who are in truth merely slaves, are called J-son's, because they are Jezebel's sons. They all parrot the same lying words coming forth from the same spirit of divination even as Jezebel does.

THE CHURCH FROM SHINAR

Multitudes of people, walking in sin and compromise, who have not yet repented of their wicked ways, are walking under delusion, and they are looking for guidance because they cannot hear the Lord, and where do they go - straight into the devils lair. They go to the churches that were built in Shinar, and they turn to the high places that have been lifted up in Babylon. That strategy is going to bring nothing but disaster to everyone who follows this path.

I suggest that we stop and reconsider what we are all doing here. We should begin following the admonitions of the Lord. If we want to restore our walk with God, and get back to the intimate place of fellowship with the Lord, we need to turn to the Lord and not the false prophets. The Lord calls this place, his secret hiding place, where we can be filled with the real

Holy Spirit, and walk in the anointing all day long. You can wake up in the morning filled with the Holy Spirit and hear with your ears the angels singing before the throne of God. That is the place of our safety and salvation.

That is the secret place of the Most High God and it is found in his presence and it is there, that the Lord leads you beside still waters and you walk in paths of peace. You do not have to worry about what to do; all you have to do is follow the Lord. And you do not have to worry about where you can go, or what you are going to eat, or how you will survive. You simply follow the Lamb, and the Lord will tell you, "do not worry, and be not afraid." Only in his presence can we truly be anxious for nothing, if we would just learn to hear his voice.

But the sheep in these last days, the charismatic sheep would rather get in the car and drive around and try to find a word from the Lord that would come through another man, or better yet, through a woe man. In Micah the Scripture admonishes all of us: "place no confidence in a guide, and trust not in a friend." The context of Micah 7 is clearly the last days, because Jesus quoted this chapter in his discourse in the last days in Matthew 24. Jesus quoted from this chapter which says, "seek no counsel from a guide nor trust in a friend to give you God's revelation", because they cannot help you. Oh, there are plenty of guides in the church, that would love to control you, but would the Lord send a man to give you guidance for your life, if in the word of God he told you to not look there. Of course not. So what is the point of the true prophets?

Their words are for confirmation only. God leads you directly; he is your shepherd and you are his sheep and he is going to lead each and every one of you. He may send a true prophet at times to speak a word of encouragement, a word of confirmation, but this whole model of everybody seeking all of these personal prophetic words, it is just another part of the last days deception which was prophesied to come. It is all part of the great delusion that has come down, and some of the people are so far gone, that the Lord says, "My words can no longer reach them."

LORD, LORD, WE PROPHESIED IN YOUR NAME

You can go so deep into the counterfeit, where you become so deceived by the lying and seducing spirits, now operating within you, that the word of the Lord can no longer reach you to pull you out of it. If the word of God can no longer reach you, then you have become entrapped, taken and devoured; you have been swallowed up by these evil entities, and you are not going to the kingdom. You are going to the fire.

On that day, these people are going to say, "Lord, Lord, we prophesied in your name." And the Lord is going to say to them, "You did not prophesy in my spirit. You prophesied in the spirit of *Ba'al*, and by a spirit of divination, and you deceived and destroyed my people. Depart from me you workers of iniquity in my church." There will be weeping and gnashing of teeth on that day, but the church does not like to think about that.

How terrible for these people and some of the people we know at church are in this group. Most of the so called prophets, will be found among them at the end. I do not say this flippantly, and I do not say this with anything other than sorrow. My heart cries out to you, repent, start fasting and praying. This is not going to work out the way we think. The people being saved are the ones being sanctified, everyone else that is staying in their sins are staying in deception as well. If you are not abiding in the Lord, and rather you are outside of his house, living in the outer court, you might not make it. The deceptions that are coming in the future are going to be so incredible, they will deceive many.

Look at what they have accomplished so far - the majority of the spirit filled church has been overrun by deceiving spirits where the average Christian can no longer even tell the difference. And if you cannot discern that the Kundalini anointing found today throughout much of the church is not the Holy Spirit, how do you know that your own faith is real, and not the apostasy? How can you know that you are really saved?

The Scripture says our spirit will bear witness with the Holy Spirit that we are his. Only those who have the spirit of Christ are his. But if the spirit that is operating within us is a Kundalini spirit, a counterfeit of the Holy Spirit, then are we really his at all?

There is nothing more powerful in the entire universe, than the living, breathing, life-giving word of God and nothing more desirable. If you have a Bible, put your hand on it and you will be touching the word of God. And if you can pray and enter into his presence, when you open the book and read, you will be reading the living word of God and he will speak to you through the *Rhema* power of the word.

THE WORD SPOKEN FALSELY IN THE NAME OF THE LORD

There is also nothing more dangerous, more insidious, and altogether evil than the word spoken falsely in the name of the Lord, which finds its origins within the carnal minds of men, or worse, the spirits of divination and darkness that are muttering and peeping in the night, for they have come right out of hell.

This is the ministry of death, which has been appointed to the false prophets, and many of them have come in the spirit of Jezebel. We all know the story of the ancient Queen, and that this spirit was in the church at the time of the writing of the book of Revelation. The Lord rebuked it, when he said, "I have a few things against you." He was speaking to his church, when he said, "you permit that woman Jezebel, who calls herself a prophetess, to teach and to seduce my servants." The church was permitting this woman, who was operating in the spirit of divination, to operate in the office of the prophetess within the church; but hers was a spirit of divination. They were permitting her a platform because they could not discern that she was a Devil, and so the Lord had to rebuke them, and tell them she is only calling herself a prophetess, for she was a diviner, operating with the spirit of deceit within her. She was divining the future for people, and seducing them.

The word for *seduce* is *plaano,* and it means to cause people to wander away from the faith, to depart from truth, and to go astray. She was also causing people to commit *fornication,* and the word is *pornea,* which means things that are unclean; this includes witchcraft, idolatry, and pornography, fornication and adultery. She was opening the door to witchcraft within the church. All kinds of abominations fall into the category of the word *pornea*, for that is the true meaning of *pornea*, that which is unclean. And the spirit of Jezebel, which is operating with the spirit of divination, is seducing the people to open the door and causing them to become involved in the unclean practice of prophesying in the spirit of Ba'al in the Assembly of God.

VAIN GLORY

Would you not consider it unclean if a demon possessed person stood up in church and delivered a satanic prophecy? Of course, that is terrible. That is exactly what Jezebel was doing, she was prophesying by the power of Satan and she was causing the people of God to eat things that were being offered up to the idols of pride. She came in the power of darkness seeking her vain glory and the people were eating the unclean things; it is not that Jezebel was bringing unclean food to the potluck, or food that she had secretly sacrificed to an idol, but rather she was leading the people to eat the very sacrifices of pride and idolatry through her deception, because they too, were now offering things to idols through their own hearts.

They had come under the spell of the divination spirit, and they were now speaking in the darkness, and engaging in the very same idolatry. In the book of Corinthians Paul tells us: "that, which has been sacrificed to an idol, is nothing", and if eaten by someone who is pure, all things remain pure. But here, in eating the thing sacrificed to the idols, they were actually engaging in the very practice of bringing offerings to the idol, for they were engaging in the same practices of receiving and giving these false words and now seducing one another.

THE COUNTERFEIT RELIGIOUS SPIRITS

The satanic counterfeit comes as a religious spirit, and it operates under the power of religious deception. Once religious demons come in, it is almost impossible to break their hold off the life of a person, because of the very nature of faith. Someone who has a religious spirit now has placed their faith in the doctrines of devils. The seducing spirits along with all of their deceptions, brought a false form of Christianity, which the deceived have now received through faith. They believe they received an anointing and a touch from God, and that all of their false doctrines are true.

They did receive an anointing, just not from God, for they received a touch from a lying spirit, and powerful religious demons have now come upon them. They believe they have the truth and they have their Bible to back them up. They also have their faith, and now that they have placed their faith in lies, their faith leaves no room for doubt in their mind. At this point, they are almost beyond hope, for only God can reach them now, and normally only through some major trauma, because he has to put them into the furnace in order to break down this false religious system or they will be gospel hardened where you cannot reach them at all.

What exactly do we have faith in? Is our faith in our opinion of ourselves? Do we place our faith in the fact that we think we have an anointing? Do we have faith in the fact that we raised our hand, and said the sinner's prayer? Do we place our faith in the words that the false prophets speak? In the major charismatic churches, they are constantly giving out these words, one to another. I am here to tell you, what passes for prophecy in this hour in most churches is almost exclusively the work of a spirit of divination or the projection of self and it is almost never from the Lord.

So, what exactly do we place our faith in? Faith in the prophetic words we received? Or do we place our faith in our knowledge of the Bible, and in religious doctrines which were created through the knowledge of good and evil as men read the Bible through their mind of the flesh? We take a leap of faith when we trust in our own understanding, and when we place our faith in our knowledge of good and evil. Yet all of us have such confidence, even certainty that surely our faith is true, for we have all learned to trust in our own understanding. Yet many people have a twisted sort of faith, buried deep within the dark places of their hearts, which are the habitations of cruelty, where they rely on their own deceptions and believe that their lying words are somehow true, and that their false faith, will somehow save them, from their fate.

There are many people who believe that the lie works. For some reason, they think they are exempt from the word of God. And that they are so special, they can lie to themselves, and they can also lie to God, and not only will it work, they believe they are going to be blessed, because they are going to get what they want.

THE CONGREGATION OF THE DEAD

These are the hallmarks of the congregation of the dead. Our faith should be in God alone and our only confidence in his eternal word of truth. And every word of truth is confirmed by two or more witnesses. If you learn anything from this book, then learn this: until a word is confirmed by two or more witnesses, you do not receive it. Because if you do, you will have committed what the Scripture calls "presumptuous sin." You just *presumed* that a certain word came from the Lord. Listen to me, there are many voices out there, and many voices have been raised up, and most of them are not from the Lord.

Jesus warned that, "many would come in my name and deceive many." The attack against you is through a massive counterfeit, and to a great extent, the deceptions of the enemy within the church are all based upon the counterfeit. A large number of false prophets have come, just as Jesus told us they would. If you get a word, something you think might be from God, you should wait for confirmation, pray and test it in the spirit. You should also search it out and see if it be so in the word of God. If the confirmation does not come, then you do not receive the word. You can put it in the *maybe* category, and maybe it will be confirmed later. Presumptuous sin is as serious as any, especially if you take action and make decisions based on some word you thought was from God and it turns out you were wrong.

What exactly is this faith, in which we have chosen to believe? And what exactly is this silk, where in the fabric of our minds, we find the spider webs we weave? To the extent we are walking in pride, we have an open door for the deceptions of the enemy. The sin of pride is an abomination before the Lord. It is a sin area that is a stronghold in many and it has been dedicated to Satan. He is the King over all of the sons of pride, and to the extent you still have some of the old Adamic pride inside, you have given a house key to the enemy. Whenever that spirit of pride rises up in you, when you are offended or someone challenges your pride, you can be certain that what you are responding in, is fully contaminated by the darkness.

All of the sons of pride commit sins of pride, for Satan is the king over all the children of pride. And all of their false words, in the end, fall to the ground and die. All these vain words create is false hope, and as the years go by, nothing comes of these false words. But I am here to tell you something did come from the false words; confusion and distraction came, and a waste of time occurred. A mindset of deception was erected in the mind of the church, that we should somehow look for words for guidance, and that we should seek out the words of men in order to find the word of God. The Lord told you himself, "Do not follow them when they tell you he is in the east at Lakeland, do not go there. If they say to you, he is in Toronto, do not go there. The coming of the kingdom of God is within." You must learn to seek the Lord yourself, and do not turn to the spirits that peep and mutter in the night.

SHE CALLS HERSELF A PROPHETESS

That woman Jezebel, she called herself a prophetess, and to those who receive her lying words, she says, "I am your spiritual mother." To the men and women that she takes captive as slaves, she calls them her children. She lifts herself up as a spiritual authority, and presents herself as a mother, but she is actually a hunter and they are merely her prey. She also calls herself a pastor, or a teacher, and surely she believes. In 100% of the cases that I have seen, that woman Jezebel believes, she is a real prophet. She feels entitled to dominate the people because she is more important than they are. She is entitled to do whatever she wants, to snare the people under her authority and control them from behind the shadows, because she knows best anyway. She is entitled to dominate the church, and she is entitled to do everything she does, because all of her wicked deeds, in her own eyes, are altogether righteous and true.

And if you cross her, she will turn and to tear you to pieces, because she is actually a predator. She is an animal from the other side. The spirit that is in the false prophet is actually deadly. Any area of our heart or mind that is not surrendered to Jesus Christ as Lord is vulnerable to satanic attack. Any part of your life, your mind or your heart that has not been placed on the altar and has not been consecrated to Jesus Christ is vulnerable to becoming an open door. The primary strategy of the enemy against you is deception. He wants to deceive you, before he destroys you, because otherwise he cannot. And deliverance from deception and from deceiving spirits is only possible through repentance. Yet repentance is only achievable through humility, so if we continue in our high minded self-image, believing that we are something, when in truth we are all nothing, confident in how important we are, or how special we are, we will not be able to come out of the deception.

These lying spirits, they tell every one of us, "You are the special one, you have unique insight, or you are one of the two witnesses, for you understand things the others do not." They want to cause every one of us to be lifted up in our own eyes, so that repentance is impossible for us, because in receiving these lies about how great we are, we become bound in our pride. The demons will then bring a fantasy world, where you imagine all the wonderful works you will one day do for the Lord, and the false prophets will come and repeat them for you. The spirits of divination will tell you, "One day you will be great. One day your name will be right next to Jesus' name. One day you will fill the stadiums, and the people will all come to hear from you." And the people begin to create an imaginary world in their minds where ultimately they will have all the glory and what they are really doing is lifting up an idol of pride in their own minds which they are unknowingly worshiping. Those meditations of all the great things which one day will be done through their hand are nothing more than the vain worship of the idol of self. And that worship is defended by a host of pride and denial, and once this deception enters within, false faith quickly hardens the resolve. The victim, now hopelessly bound, is held fast and strong by the religious spirits of deception that are now within. It takes major prayer and fasting to break this stuff off.

THE ULTIMATE DECEPTION

Unless our thought structures change, through genuine repentance, deliverance can be impossible. And that is never truer than when we have been overcome by religious spirits, and they are everywhere today. They are the ultimate deception confronting a Christian, because Satan is not going to get very far trying to tempt a believer to go smoke pot or go sit in a bar and get drunk, because most Christians have no interest in these things. So Satan is not going to tempt you with obviously wicked things, but the religious spirits, they come to you with the fruit from the tree of the knowledge of good and evil, and it is desirable in your eyes, for this fruit can make you wise, and then it can all be yours. You can speak the words of power, and you can be the one lifted up. You can have the great ministry, and you can have all of the money too. And you can have all the people following you. All you have to do is believe, and then just receive it, and let it come inside of your heart which is now filled with pride and then you just opened wide the door for the demons to come inside. If the Lord does not later deliver you, that day, was the day you died.

I am astonished at what I see. Genuine repentance is almost impossible when you have been overcome by religious demons. That is why the people who operate with a divination spirit, the false prophets, are not open to a word of correction. You can tell them, they have a spirit of divination operating in them, and you are not going to get a positive response out of most of these false prophets; rather they will turn and dash you to pieces. It is very unlikely that any of them will listen, and say, "would you pray for me." More likely they will run you right out of their church. The spirits of divination are powerful, because they operate through the will of the victim, and they are almost automatic to the false prophets every beck and call. They are spontaneous and always ready, with another word for you.

DECEIVING AND BEING DECEIVED

For many shall come in my name, saying "I am anointed" and they shall deceive many. The word for *deceive* means to seduce. "Evil men and seducers shall wax worse and worse, deceiving and being deceived." These people are themselves deceived. The ones that are bringing this deception into the church think they have found the truth. They have the special truth, where they are always the superstar; they are always the person with the revelation. God has chosen them for some special-purpose, and so, in being lifted up, they are more than willing to give voice to the muttering spirits of darkness. Seducers will wax worse and worse, and the word for *seducers* means; an imposter or a wizard muttering spells and enchantments. These seducers are actually wizards, and they are operating in the power of witchcraft, for they are diviners, who operate with divination spirits and so they can foretell the future. And they can be accurate, for a season, in order for you to gain confidence in them and put your trust in their words, and then they give you the words of death, that are designed to kill you. After they gain your confidence, they slaughter you, and they rob you of everything. They steal everything of value and then they put you in a body bag when they are done.

Their first step is to gain your confidence, so they initially may appear legitimate but they are actually speaking spells with evil intent, for the false prophets are imposters and seducers and their false words of knowledge and their false prophecies are darkening everything they touch. And this is everywhere around you; this is the terrible time Jesus warned us would come at the end of the age. The strongholds from these seducers have created a pattern of thinking in the minds of many that is not biblical. These deceptions have been created through twisted words that the enemy brings to slay the people of God, and to put you in a prison of deception, which is built within the minds of men. Satan is imprisoning you, with in your mind, through the doctrines of devils that you received in the false prophetic words that you believed. And that brought great devastation and destruction upon you, and most cannot even see this. At a minimum, they separated you from your God, especially if you began to follow them. And the answer is to return to the Lord, and to renounce these words, and to forsake them. To choose what you are going to believe, for the simpleminded believe every word, but the prudent man looks well to his going.

> *And he said unto me, Son of man, go unto the house of Israel, and speak my words to them. But the house of Israel will not listen to you; for they will not listen to me: for all the house of Israel are impudent and hard hearted. Ezekiel 3:4,7*

They are stubborn and loud, and stiff hearted. The word for *impudent* is חזק, *châzâq*, and it means; strong in a bad sense, hard, impudent, loud and stiff hearted. And the word for *hard hearted* is קשה, *qâsheh* and it means; cruel, grievous, stiff necked, obstinate and stubborn.

> *So the spirit lifted me up, and took me away, and I went in bitterness in the heat of my spirit; and the hand of the LORD was strong upon me. Ezekiel 3:8*

The word for *bitterness* is מרה, *mârah* and it means; heavy, angry, and discontented. The word for *heat* is חמא, *chêmâh* and it means; anger, hot displeasure, to be furious, and to be filled with rage and full of wrath.

I SAT THERE ASTONISHED FOR SEVEN DAYS

Ezekiel saw the same counterfeit in his day, and he was furious. And the hand of the Lord was strong upon him. "Then I came to them of the captivity at Tel Aviv, that dwelt by the river of Chebar, and I sat where they sat, and remained there astonished among them seven days."[42] What has happened to Israel in the natural, where they were taken into captivity to Babylon as slaves, for their sin and compromise, has happened to the Christian church in the spirit. Because of the sin and compromise in the church, the Lord has allowed the churches in America to be taken into captivity spiritually. So you can go and sit among the captives, only they do not know they are enslaved. Tel Aviv was a city of "Green Mountains", a city built in Babylon, and the river Chebar is a river where the water is soiled and dirty, a river with muddy water in it.

While I was preparing this study, I had an open, waking vision; and I saw the word of God in a dry wilderness, like a desert with the ground parched and cracked, like a seabed that had completely dried. And the word of God was there; wide open with a bright light upon it. And then suddenly, a huge serpent came up out of the cracks of the earth and began to move back and forth behind the word. And I sat there watching this, astonished. How could people replace the word of God with doctrines of devils? Do you think I imagined this in my mind? It was prophesied to come.

MEN SHALL NO LONGER ENDURE SOUND DOCTRINE

Men shall no longer endure sound doctrine, rather they shall be turned to fables, fairytales made up in the imagination of the minds of men for the itching ears, and they shall satisfy themselves and gather together many false teachers to teach them pleasant things, doctrines of demons, and prophetic words right out of hell: And it comes forth as a serpent coming up out of the earth, which is where the false prophet of the book of Revelation comes from. The beast rises up out of the sea, while the false prophet comes up out of the earth, and he comes forth with the Scriptures in his hand, and he comes with a prophetic word in his mouth.

> *Then the spirit entered into me and set me on my feet and spoke with me and he said go shut itself within your house but know son of man, they shall try to put their bands on you, and they shall try to bind you with them, but you will not go out among them anymore.*

And that word for *shut* means to enclose yourself. I have literally done this. I shut myself in my house and I did not go out among them anymore. And then I broke their bands off of me. And I suggest you do the same. "I sat there astonished for all that I had seen, and all that I had heard among them." The word for *astonished* is שׁמם, *shâmêm* and it means; to be stunned and devastated, to be utterly amazed and to sit in astonishment, in a desolate place and to see the destruction and to utterly wonder.

SANCTIFY THE LORD OF HOSTS HIMSELF

> *Sanctify the LORD of hosts himself; and let him be your fear, and let him be your dread. And he shall be for a sanctuary; but for a stone of stumbling and for a rock of offence to both the houses of Israel, for a gin and for a snare to the inhabitants of Jerusalem. And many among them shall stumble, and fall, and be broken, and be snared, and be taken. Isaiah 8:13-15*

Sanctify the Lord alone; sanctify the Lord first and above everything. Seek the Lord, and let everything else go. This one thing we must do, return to the Lord with all of our hearts. Nothing else matters. Let the Lord be your fear, and let him be your dread. If you sanctify the Lord and you put the Lord first, he shall become a sanctuary for you. If you seek him with all your might and all your strength and if he becomes your fear and your dread, then he shall become a sanctuary for you in the days that are ahead.

But if not, you will find a stone of stumbling and a rock of offense in your path, and a gin and a snare for all the inhabitants of the churches in America. And many of you will stumble, and the word for *many* is רב, *rab* which means; exceedingly full, very many, or virtually all. Virtually all of you are going to stumble, and the word for *stumble* is כּשל, *kaw-shal'* and it means to waiver and to falter, to be cast down and be ruined, to be overthrown and be caused to stumble, to become utterly weak and to fall down.

MANY HAVE STUMBLED AND FALLEN

Many are going to stumble, and when they stumble, some are going to *fall*, נפל, *nâphal* and it means; to be judged, to be cast away, to be overwhelmed, and to be overthrown and to be thrown down and perish. And others will stumble and then be broken, and the word for *broken* is שׁבר, *shaw-bar'* and it means; to be broken into pieces, to be hurt, to be crushed and become broken hearted. You are not going to perish; you are just going to have your outer man broken into pieces. And the breaking of the outer man will produce a breaking of your hearts, which will lead you to true repentance, and there the Lord will restore you.

And some of you when you stumble and fall will be snared and taken. And to be snared literally means to be snared with the fowler's snare, where deceiving spirits came in and set a snare for you, and you walked right into it, but the Lord can deliver you. The Lord can pull that snare right out of your life, and right off your foot. If you have been snared, there is hope for you yet, if you return to the Lord.

But then there are those that are *taken*, in the Hebrew word is לכד, *law-kad'* and it means; to have been captured, and fully occupied, caught in a pit as if frozen. These are the people that have been turned over and taken by the evil ones, and they actually believe they are operating in the anointing, but there is deep wickedness within. If they would search their hearts and disclose what lies deep within, they would admit that they were lying and deceiving, and hunting the people of God for their ego and for their own gain.

THIS KIND ONLY COMES OUT THROUGH FASTING AND PRAYER

So, if you do not sanctify the Lord, and seek first the kingdom of God, if you do not humble yourself, and you cannot fast and pray, you are never going to break all the snares and bondages off of your life. This kind only comes out through fasting and prayer, so if you do not fast and pray, then you are likely to stumble on the stumbling stone. The vast majority will stumble, and when you stumble you are going to fall, and be judged, or be broken and then led to true repentance, or you will be snared in a need of deliverance, yet there remains hope for you, or you will be simply taken away by the darkness, and you will not be coming back.

If you stumble and fall, and God allows you to be broken, that was his abiding mercy upon your life. He lets these deceptions which came in through your compromise, ultimately bring about repentance through a broken heart. In the remnant which God is sanctifying in this hour, the Lord is number one in their life, and they put it all on the altar, and they take it all to the cross. That is the remnant.

Everybody else has something they want to hide or something they want to hold onto, which gives the enemy ground. To the extent you do not take everything to the cross, you keep a little bit of the flesh nature alive. You still walk in a little of that pride, or you keep a little of that gluttony, or you want a little bit of that impure sex, a little of that pornography, to keep those things from Babylon, and still use those things of the flesh.

If you still want to run with them, you will find they only run to perdition, and you will have opened yourself up to the lie and the truth of God will no longer be a sanctuary for you. Rather it will now become a stone of stumbling, and a rock of offense in your life, and you will stumble. If the Lord still finds some good things in your heart, then you are going to fall down and be broken. And in your breaking, you are going to cry out in pain, and throw away your idols, and then you will seek the Lord with your whole heart, and then he is going to snatch you right out of the hand of the beast and then hide you in his secret hiding place. He is going to give you shelter from the storm, but if you are altogether corrupted by the sin you have let within, then you will be taken, and for some, they will not be coming back.

THE FEAR OF THE LORD IS THE BEGINNING OF WISDOM

The fear of the Lord is the beginning of wisdom. If you have not yet feared the Lord, and I do not mean knowledge of the fear of the Lord, I am talking about the actual fear of the Lord when you realize you can deceive yourself. There could be something in us all that is so offensive, that the Lord lets us stumble, and we would not even know it. And that is terrifying. The sin within all of us is so deceptive, for the human heart is deceitfully wicked and no man knows it.

There are multitudes of people who, on that day, are going to say, "Lord, Lord." Jesus told us many would say "we cast out devils in your name. We prophesied in your name, we did the power works in your name. We were walking in the Holy Spirit. We even prophesied to each other all day long, nice prophetic words." Jesus is going to say to the many of them, "I never knew you." These people are going to hell. I don't know about you, but I have seriously considered what it might mean to go to hell. I do not wish it on my enemies. I am not capable of doing it myself. I thank the Lord I am not going there, because I could not handle it. I would miss the Lord too much, and I could not handle the fire.

I will tell you what the fear of the Lord is like: with the fear of the Lord, you take his word seriously enough that when you read in the book of Joel that God commanded us to declare a solemn assembly, call the elders and fast and pray, you actually start fasting. You do not just think about it. You actually do it. And then when the anointing comes, because when you do fast and pray, you get the breakthrough, and if you get a little hungry after a few days, you are afraid to eat, until God says the fast is over. You are afraid to move without the Lord's authorization, because you know how deceitful your own heart is, for it can deceive you and you could do something to offend the Lord and not even know you did. That is a reason to be afraid. The fear of the Lord is the beginning of wisdom, and it will cause you to depart from evil.

> *And when they shall say unto you, Seek unto them that have familiar spirits, and unto wizards that peep, and that mutter: should not a people seek unto their God? for the living to the dead? Isaiah 8:19*

And when they say unto you, go and hear the word of the latest prophet who has come to give personal prophetic words to everyone, stop and think before you go and listen to them. For the word for *seek* is דרש, *dârash,* and it means; frequently, following and asking, and diligently inquiring of a necromancer, a spiritist. The word for *wizards* is ידעני, *yiddehonee,* and it means; a conjurer, or a witch or a ghost. Why do the people of God turn to evil spirits for advice? King Saul sought out the witch of Endor, after the spirit of the Lord abandoned him, and after Samuel was gone. Saul went to the witch of Endor, but it did not profit him at all.

A TIME OF DARKNESS HAD COME

It is a time of extreme darkness when the people of God look to seducers, and wizards, for the light they need to guide their path in order to find a way that they should go for themselves and their families. What an unnatural thing that the very

Church of God would go and inquire, not of the Lord, but seeking other men and women, who in truth are but false prophets, the very false prophets Jesus warned us would come. These are demonic deceivers, and the people that went and inquired of them, are the most to be pitied. To inquire of a man in this hour, when the Lord said place no-confidence in a guide, is the height of foolishness and absolute folly. What blindness, why consult the dead for the interest of the living?

Why turn to the spirits of death for instruction of God's saints? This is one of the greatest and darkest deceptions ever. The Lord's response to this insanity is in Isaiah 8:20 where he said, "to the law and to the testimony of the prophets of God", the prophets whose words are recorded in Holy Scripture, "if they speak not according to this word, it is because there is no light in them." That is another test of whether you are dealing with a false prophet.

But the people would not seek the Lord, instead they turned and sought counsel from the false prophets, and the counsel of the dead. To them the Scripture says, "and they shall pass through the land, hungry and in hardships, and it will come to pass that they will fret, and they shall worry and be filled with anxiety, and then they will curse their king and their God, and they will look upward and they shall look under the earth and they will behold only trouble in darkness, and dimness of anguish, and they shall be driven to darkness."

A night of despair is coming upon this unbelieving nation and upon its apostate church which has turned to blind guides for their light. These people will wander about in a land that is cursed and will become hungry because all provisions will be gone, the fields and the vineyards will be laid to waste. An apostate church, which refused to fast and pray, will now experience real hunger for the first time, and in the gnawing agony that will grow in their flesh, they will work themselves into a rage, then they will curse their king and they will curse their fate and they will curse the god they fashioned in their minds, which was merely just an idol of pride. They curse the idol of their pride, which they made and chose as their god, cursing their wretched fate without discerning the justice of the punishment they are receiving for their part in the apostasy and for never humbling themselves in repentance.

The people, who go all the way in following the false prophets, end up in the darkness, and at that point, do they turn to the Lord? No. They never do humble themselves, and they never repent. Finally they are fasting because they are starving to death, but they are unable to repent and so they are unable to humble themselves, consequently all their rage and their wrath avails them nothing. They turn their eyes upwards and they only see blackened skies, which are darkening all the more. They look to the earth, and everywhere they find nothing but distress and darkness and a night of anguish all about them.

THE FALSE PROPHETS HAVE MADE MANY WIDOWS

Who are these people that are deceived by the false prophets? This is a serious problem and this is going to cause the loss of people's lives. The Scripture says the false prophets made many widows in the land of Israel. False prophets can kill you. They can kill your family, and they can destroy your life. It is like taking up a serpent in your hands, now you might like snakes, but these things can bite you. If you hold them long enough, then you will get bitten, and many times, the bites are actually fatal.

Let us look at the false prophets that lead entire congregation's right into hell. The people look to these deceiving spirits, and then hang on their every word. As I was preparing this study, the Lord gave me a dream in which I saw a man wrapped up and sewn into a large sock pillow and it was orange in color, much like a sock puppet with a man inside. It appeared before me, and I pushed my hand into the back, and it began to tear open, and then I heard a voice say: "To Jason, and to Satan and the women and to all those creating all of the commotion in the isles."

Five things were revealed in this dream: Jason, Satan, the women, and every one creating all the commotion which is occurring in the isles. We know who Satan is, and we are well aware of his game. He has Jason, and the women, and a lot of other volunteers, who are all doing his bidding, and they are creating all of the *commotion*, and it is happening in a place called the *isles*. So let us study this like Bereans, and see if this dream came from the Lord, and if it is confirmed by two or more witnesses. First, let us start with the action, and leave the actors for the second part of the study. Let us look at the word commotion, it turns out the word appears only one time in the Scriptures.

> *Woe is me for my hurt! my wound is grievous: but I said, Truly this is a grief, and I must bear it. My tabernacle is spoiled, and all my cords are broken: my children are gone forth of me, and they are not: there is none to stretch forth*

my tent any more, and to set up my curtains. For the pastors are become brutish, and have not sought the LORD: therefore they shall not prosper, and all their flocks shall be scattered. Behold, the noise of the bruit is come, and a great commotion out of the North Country, to make the cities of Judah desolate, and a den of dragons.
Jeremiah 10:19-22

THE PASTORS HAVE BECOME BRUTISH

The pastors have become brutish, for they have not sought the Lord. Therefore they shall not prosper, and all their flocks shall be scattered. "Behold the noise of the brute has come, and a great commotion out of the North Country to make the cities of Judah desolate and a den of Dragons." This all happened once before, in the ancient land of Israel, and there, the pastors all became brutish, and as a result, the congregation turned into a great commotion, and in the end, the cities were destroyed and the land became a den of dragons.

What does it mean to become *brutish*? The word is בער, *ba᷾ar* and it means; to set ablaze by fire, and to burn. The English definition of brutish is to be brutal, or to be cruel, and to become carnal resembling a beast; to become coarse, showing little intelligence and lacking any understanding. It is the French word for *noise*. It is a brutal, insensitive, cruel and crude person who has the nature of the beast: they are irrational, and no longer characterized by reason, rather their behavior can be defined as clamoring, or roaring as they spread rumors.

In the congregation where this great commotion is occurring, the people have turned into something resembling a beast. The gentleness, and lovingkindness which are fruit of the Holy Spirit, are gone. Now what you find is a congregation of people that are actually cruel. The Scripture tells us the dark places of the earth are the habitations of cruelty, and in the congregations which have become darkened, there you find the brute; where the pastors have become brutish, and the people have become like the beast, and together they are all creating all of this commotion.

The word *commotion* רעש, *ra'ash;* it is defined as; confusing noise, quaking and shaking. Is that not what the false prophets bring? Confusing noise, with their false words of knowledge, they bring a state of noisy and confused activity. While the people are falling down, and twitching as in an epileptic seizure, while the demons are affixing themselves to the spinal cord of their prey.

Commotion creates a state of mental excitement, but one filled with only confusion and agitation, while the setting turns into a social disturbance filled with upheaval, sedition and insurrection. These are all the definitions of the word commotion. The commotion has created a disturbance in the church, and agitation and confusion in the minds of the people, who now bring only sedition and insurrection against God's proper order. A synonym for commotion is *pandemonium*, which is the name of the capital of hell. This Jason character, and the women that are under the influence of Satan, and all the people that are being animated by the spirit of rebellion, all of this wickedness within the church is creating a commotion, and when it is in full swing, the churches resemble pandemonium, the capital of hell.

THOSE WHO DWELL CARELESSLY IN THE ISLES

Now let us look at the word for isles. This is where it starts getting really interesting. The word *isle* appears in the Scripture in several locations. One of them is Ezekiel 39:6: "And I will send a fire on Magog, and among them that dwell carelessly in the ***isles***." The word for *isles* in Hebrew is the letters Aleph and Yod, **אי**, and it is pronounced *eye* and it means a desirable spot, but also a dry land, an island, or a land that is separated, and divided.

The actual word in the text of this Scripture is **איים** , pronounced *Eye-eim,* which is plural for *islands* but this word is also a negative particle. Standing alone in Hebrew, aleph-yod is almost never used because it is a negative particle, it always means the anti or negative of whatever follows. If you were to say Messiah in Hebrew, and if you placed aleph-yod in front of Messiah, you just said antichrist. Aleph-yod means anti or the negative and it is the word for that which stands opposed.

The *isles,* where everyone is creating only a commotion, is the dry land where everybody speaks in the negative. It is the land of negative thinking and where the critical and the judgmental Christians walk in the mind of the flesh and not with the Lord. It is a dry land where people only speak curses, and were much of the conversation involves slander; it is also a land where the pastors have become brutish, and the people are only focused on the things which please the beast nature of the flesh, while they disregard the things of the Lord. And it is a land in which the spirit of Jezebel is running rampant.

The majority of the men who dwell there are called *"Jay's sons."* What is also interesting, aleph yod, which is the word for anti or negative, is also defined as a land that is divided by strife and contention, which the lying spirits bring into the church. Thus aleph-yod is translated as an island, a land that is separated, and thus divided. The letters אי are also part of the word in Hebrew for *man* איש, which is pronounced *eash,* and it is spelled aleph-yod followed by the letter shin, ש.

The letter ש shin in Hebrew is a picture of the fire of the presence of God in the Holy Spirit coming down and burning the offering of flesh upon the brazen altar; it is the 21st letter in the Hebrew alphabet, and represents the number 777 which means perfection. It is also the number 300 in Hebrew and its ancient meaning is the Cosmic Fire of the Holy Spirit which comes down from above. There are three parts to this fire, representing the triune presence of Almighty God. So the word for *man* in Hebrew, pronounced *Ish,* means "one without the Holy Spirit" or "no holy spirit from above." It is a man in the flesh, and his very nature is opposed to the things of God. The root word of Aleph-yod, also means a dry land, a land that is cursed with famine, a land of no water, where the double portion of the curse is a drought of no rain in the natural and no rain in the spirit, and thus, there is no word from God.

OPPOSED TO THE HOLY SPIRIT

The word for ***man*** in Hebrew means a *man in the flesh* who is devoid of, and opposed to, the Holy Spirit. In other words, the Hebrew word for man means the men of the flesh who are utterly opposed to the Holy Spirit, and the word for ***man*** reveals to us that the flesh itself is opposed to the Holy Spirit. Is this meaning in Hebrew doctrinally correct? Is it true that the flesh opposes the Holy Spirit?

The Hebrew word for man means a man in the flesh who is devoid of the Holy Spirit and hence is opposed to all the things of God. This is the *isles* in which all of this commotion is occurring. The spirit of divination is there, and the spirits of condemnation and slavery are there as well.

Let's talk about the other characters in the dream, which dwell in this dry land: Jason and the women, and all the other folks who are creating all of this commotion in the flesh. This is the church which is full of people who are all walking in the flesh, doing what is right in their eyes, but they are not being led by the Spirit of God. So rather than bringing a sacrifice of praise, the Lord said, "these only bring a sacrifice of strife and contention in my house." It is where they contend with one another, and strive with each other, and it is a hideous situation. This dry land is a land that is cursed, and there has been a famine for the true word of God in this land for many years. There is a drought of living water in this land, so that it has become a very dry land. There is no water and rather there is a double portion of the curse. No rain in the natural and no rain in the spirit. That is the picture of a land filled with divination and deception, where the hearts of the people bring only an offering of strife and contention in his house. But they have many prophets speaking warm, inviting and uplifting words to comfort the hearts which have long ago, grown so cold to the things of God.

What about this color orange? The man who was wrapped up in a sock pillow, it was colored orange. Orange is a warm color, it is inviting, and uplifting, spontaneous and stimulating to the appetite; orange will keep people comfortable, and talking and eating for a long time. Orange relates to a 'gut reaction' and 'gut instincts' and to social communication, and to words or conversation, but these words of orange bring only a false hope. The orange color represents the false words of the false prophets which are the boundless manna which they speak out of their gut, or the words from the divination spirits, which will also be found falling only to the ground in this dry and desolate place.

SHE CALLS THEM HER SONS

The man was literally tied in a pillow of false words and we will see in Ezekiel 13, this is exactly how the Jezebel spirit of divination works. She binds them, and sews pillows over the hands of the people; over their minds and then over the whole man, making him a slave to her will and to the divination spirit operating within her. But she calls them her sons, thus the name Jason, "J" being for Jezebel. The slaves who have been captured by the deceiving spirits which operate within her, are the *"Jason's"*, and the color of this deception is orange, for it is a warm color, inviting and uplifting, even spontaneous. There is no waiting on God here. It is stimulating to the appetite, causing you to always want more. Is that not what the false prophets do, these people that are constantly giving out these personal prophetic words, and then they get inflated images of themselves, and think they are really something. "I am really needed; all of these little people need me to guide their lives" and so the people always need to go back to the prophet.

These false prophetic words stimulate the appetite for more and more of this deception. More ropes on you and more bindings to enslave you, and that is exactly what is happening to the people who are chasing these false prophets. But the orange also keeps the people comfortable, it will keep them talking, and the demons do not care. You can talk all you want at church, they just want to make sure you hear their words and that they sink into your hearts because that is where they do the damage. Keep them talking and keep them eating the false words, which bring them hope, but only a false hope.

The pillowcases represent taking the authority or the dominion over the people, and turning them into puppets. And that big pillow that I saw looked like a sock puppet. And I would have to say the women are winning the false prophet contest because there are more women than men engaged in this activity. Maybe it is sixty forty weighing in as a win for the women. However, both sexes are well represented within the false prophet camp.

The divination spirit which has come, it claims to be infallible like the Pope. These false prophets think they are infallible, and you cannot challenge them, and they will never tell you, "test this word." They believe they are infallible and if you question anything, they will only get angry. And if the men who are false prophets think they are like the Pope, then the women must be Pope-ettes! And they are binding the people in their sock puppets. And the Jezebel Pope-ettes, they too believe they are infallible.

Who is Jason and where does that name come from anyway? The name comes from classical Greek mythology. Jason was a hero, the leader of the Argonauts, who retrieved the Golden Fleece with the help of, or under the spell of, a witch named Medea. He was a prince, a son of one a king, and he met a woman, whose name was Media and she was a witch and an enchantress; she put a spell on Jason, and took him captive. She had the gift of prophecy, for she was a diviner, and she had the spirit of divination within her. She represents Jezebel, and Jason is her victim. She takes Jason captive and marries him, using her magic powers, and she provides him advice.

THE MEDIA HAS LIFTED UP THE FALSE CHURCH

Is this not fascinating how this parallels the reality in the false church of this hour in which Jezebel steals the souls of men in this age, for she did so with the help of the "media." Today, the media lifts up the false church worldwide. Jezebel wants the glory, so she convinces Jason to lead a quest to steal the Golden Fleece which represents the crown of glory that rightfully belongs only to the King. When Jason finally comes out of his trance, and realizes the witch for the enchantress that she is, he flees from her. Once discovered, she responds in a fit of rage, and then murders all of their children.

Is it not fascinating that much of the false church, which has deceived the souls of men in this age, also did so with the help of the media. The power of the airwaves empowered these false teachers to deceive the souls of men and behind the false gospel is the spirit of false prophecy and idolatry which controls these seducers who were all sent by hell, and they are controlled by the power of the spirit of Jezebel.

She is a murderer and she did it all, for her vainglory. And the people in the church today that are operating in this same spirit are in total denial. They believe everything they are doing is of God. But we are going to see, as we get a little further along, nothing could be further from the truth.

THAT WOMAN JEZEBEL

So, who is this woman named Jezebel, who the Lord referred to as, "that woman"? Her name in Hebrew is אִיזֶבֶל, *ee-zeh'-bel*. She was the wife of Ahab, who was king of Israel in the days of Elijah. She was born a princess in Zidon, which in Hebrew means the city of pride. Her name means, no husband, no prince, no lord and under no authority. She is a picture of a woman who has rejected the covering of her husband, along with the authority of the Lord, only to then lift herself up in the place of authority. We know very little of her early life. Scripture only bears witness of the dark heart of an evil woman who ruled the throne of Israel from the shadows in her later years. By then her conscience was seared; she murdered the prophets of God with impunity and in their place, she raised up the false prophets of Ba'al to feast at her table.

The word *Ba'al* in Hebrew בַּעַל, means Lord or husband. The difference between the true prophets and the false is not the name in which they came, for the name בַּעַל, Ba'al means Lord, but the spirit which sent them among us. The *Lord* they were worshiping was another god. Jesus warned us many will come in his name and deceive many. Many came in the name of the God of Israel, and they came in the name of בַּעַל, *Ba'al*, but they were not of the Lord, for they came in the spirit of divination and they were part of Satan's deception. Although the name was the same, the God that they were serving had changed.

This spirit manifested itself within the Church in the days of the Apostles, and it received the rebuke of Jesus in his letters to the churches of the book of Revelation. And the presence of this spirit is an epidemic in the church in this last hour, when the Lord told us, many false prophets shall come, Jezebel was among them.

THE SPIRIT OF REBELLION

Jezebel represents the spirit of rebellion against all authority. She is in rebellion against the Lord, for she wants her will and none other; she wants her way or it is no way, and she wants to dominate the church, from behind the scenes. She also wants to dominate the people in her life, but this is all hidden and done in the shadows. She will not admit this, even to herself. She just wants to force her way because she knows she is right. She has the best interest of everyone in mind. She knows what to do, and she knows what to tell you to do as well. But this is all coming out of a hardened heart full of rebellion and pride.

How did she get this way? How did all of these women, that are now being dominated by a spirit of divination, get this way? Was the conscience within her darkened from birth or did the sorrows and disappointments of life turn her heart into the heart of a beast. We are only left to wonder how the anger grew within that woman Jezebel. It was set on fire by the very fires of hell, in the heart of a woman rejected and scorned; burning in envy, to take what is not hers. This is a woman who has been turned over to the darkness, and now is full of the rejection of authority, and hatred of men. Responding in kind, she rejects both men and the authority appointed by the Lord as a covering for her.

I personally know of one woman that the Lord ultimately unveiled as operating under the spirit of divination, who was told her to her face, "you received divination spirits" and you need to repent. Of course, she would not receive it, because those operating under these deceiving spirits rarely do. She used to say, "I will never trust in any *man*" with such an emphasis of disdain on the word for *man*. What it shouted is, "I hate men." And the Scripture does say, "place no confidence in men", but also place no trust in women either. For we are to place no confidence in the flesh at all, because the flesh is nothing more than that which is opposed to the Holy Spirit, and utterly opposed to the Lord. There is nothing there to be confident in.

ROOTS OF BITTERNESS

This is a woman operating with deep roots of bitterness within, and if you were to unveil it all, you would find she is angry and has not gone to the cross with her pain, rather she let the seeds of bitterness grow and now she has the heart of a beast within. Her conscience has been sealed in bitterness, and with her faith in men destroyed, her respect for all authority has turned into total disdain. Her eyes are now only full of darkness, while the heart within her has hardened in the rebellion of sin. This Princess from Zidon has been turned over to the spirit of rebellion, and is now cursed to wander the night alone and driven on by her bitterness to hunt for her prey in the dark. The weapons of her plunder are the same lying words which betray the evil hidden within her soul. Intent on stealing or to destroy, she hunts for souls as trophies, sewing them up. Her words are the declarations of darkness, where she casts up her lies like foam on the sea.

She speaks negative words of unbelief: "You will always battle this, you will never accomplish that. You can never do this and you will always need my help." Always and never are two of her favorite words, for this way, the spells and curses she binds, are meant to last an eternity. In Ezekiel chapter 13, let us look at the text which uncovers this deception:

> *And the word of the LORD came unto me, saying, Son of man, prophesy against the prophets of Israel that prophesy, and say unto them that prophesy out of their own hearts, Hear ye the word of the LORD; Woe unto the foolish prophets, that follow their own spirit, and have seen nothing! They have seen vanity and lying divination, saying, The LORD saith: and the LORD hath not sent them: and they have made others to hope that they would confirm the word. Ezekiel 13:1-6*

They prophesy as if the Lord said, but the Lord did not send them. They say, "I got this from the Lord", but no they did not. And they cause others to hope that they would confirm the false words. Several of these deceivers can confirm the false words one for another, but it is still not the Lord. And the Lord said unto them, because you see vanity and speak lies, "I am against you."

My hand shall be upon the prophets that see vanity, and that divine lies: they shall not be in the assembly of my people, neither shall they be written in the writing of the house of Israel, nor shall they enter into the land of Israel; and you shall know that I am the Lord your God. Ezekiel 13:9

I HAVE SEEN YOUR LIES

I wonder if the writings which the Lord is referring, includes the book of life. If these false prophets operating in a spirit of divination, have not erased their name from the Lamb's book of life. The Lord says, "I have seen your lies, and therefore I am against you. I have seen your vanity and that you divine lies." They are using divination; they are not just making it up. An evil spirit from hell has come into them and they use the power of that evil spirit to weave their lies.

The Lord speaks against the false prophets saying, "because they have seduced my people, saying, Peace; and there was no peace; and one built up a wall, and, lo, others daubed it with un-tempered mortar."[43] The false prophets operate as a tag team; one builds the walls of false prophecy, and another dubs it with un-tempered mortar. Then the Lord says, "I will even rend this wall that you build with a stormy wind in my fury; and there shall be an overflowing shower in mine anger, and great hailstones in my fury to consume it. So will I break down the wall that ye have daubed with un-tempered mortar, and bring it down to the ground, so that the foundation thereof shall be discovered, and it shall fall, and ye shall be consumed in the midst thereof: and ye shall know that I am the LORD."[44]

"I will accomplish my wrath on that wall a false prophecy, and upon them that build and daubed it." If you worked on this project, the wrath of God is coming on you too. These are the walls of deception, the walls of division, and these are the walls that enslaved the people of God in the prisons created by the false prophets that sought to rule over them. They were capturing the people within these walls; this was the path to the acquisition of power for the false prophet. These people claim they have heard from the Lord, and who can top that? And then they just start giving orders to everybody. "The Lord said you should do this and the Lord said you should do that. And all of you should give me your money, a faith offering of good seed in this good soil. God told me someone here is going to give me $1,000 tonight."

THE WRATH OF GOD SHALL COME

So, the wrath of God is going to come upon all of this, and God says, "I will accomplish my wrath upon this wall, so that the wall will be no more, and neither will they be that daubed it." You do not want anything to do with false prophecy or the false prophets. You should run from them. And bear in mind, they are operating under a deceiving spirit, so being deceived they will defend their ministry of death until the end, when they too shall die.

> *Likewise, thou son of man, set thy face against the daughters of thy people, which prophesy out of their own heart; and prophesy thou against them, And say, Thus saith the Lord God; Woe to the women that sew pillows to all armholes, and make kerchiefs upon the head of every stature to hunt souls! Will ye hunt the souls of my people,*

and will ye save the souls alive that come unto you? And will ye pollute me among my people for handfuls of barley and for pieces of bread, to slay the souls that should not die, and to save the souls alive that should not live, by your lying to my people that hear your lies? Ezekiel 13:17-19

The Lord now commands the prophet Ezekiel to turn his face against the daughters of Israel, who have been prophesying out of their own hearts as well. The first thing we learn is the false prophets are prophesying out of their own heart, and not out of the mind of the Lord. And the Lord speaks, "Woe unto to the women that sew pillows over the armholes and over the hands of my people and make veils for the head of every statue, to hunt the souls there with."

TAKING AUTHORITY OVER THE PEOPLE

The words for *armholes* in Hebrew is two words, אצּיל, *ats-tseel* and יד, *yad*, which mean; a covering of the hand, and the word for *hand* means power, and strength, and authority. So these false prophets want to sew up the hand of power and authority in the lives of people. Think of it as putting a mitten on the hands of a small baby so he cannot scratch his face. But he also cannot use his thumb, so he cannot use his hands. The false prophets have taken away the power of God in your life, because you have to keep relying on them. You cannot hear from the Lord yourself, you have to keep going back to them. They hear better than you do, so they treat you like children and sew mittens on your hands. And they put veils upon every head, and the veil is the veil of deception, in which they cover up what they are doing to the people. It is as if they are claiming as property, the slaves which they have just captured.

God's people are supposed to be free, and under the direction of the Lord, and these people are sewing them up as a sock puppet, and capturing them. They want to put you on their prophetic Facebook page, so they can exalt themselves: "I have all these people who listen to me and they are tied to me as well." They also do it for the *corn,* and the Scripture says, "will you hunt the souls of my people?" And that word for *hunt* is צוּד, *tsûd,* and it means; to catch a man, to lie in wait, and it is through deceit that they hunt. The Lord says unto them, "will ye pollute me among my people for handfuls of barley and for pieces of bread, to slay the souls that should not die, and to save the souls alive that should not live, by your lying to my people that hear your lies?"[45]

The word for *pollute* means; to profane, to defile or to prostitute. "Are you going to prostitute my word for a handful of corn?" Are you going to use a supposed word from God for profit? Notice they slay the souls that should not die, and the word for *profane* means; to pollute and hold in contempt or irreverence what is sacred. Think about this; the word of God is sacred. If the Lord should show us grace, to actually speak to us, and you knew you actually heard from God, and you could write down what he said, and put it in quotes, as I have in my books, and you could tell everybody, I have heard from the Lord, and the Lord said thus and so, that is as sacred as it gets. These false prophets, they make it up as they go, and actually a spirit of divination is driving them on to take the word of the Lord and counterfeit it, in order to take people into slavery and take In order to take the control of the church, manipulate the pastor, and to exercise dominion over people, so that their will would be done on earth as it is in the imagination of their minds.

They will take the most precious gift we have, which is the word of the Lord, for it is the most powerful and sacred, holy piece of heaven to ever come within this fallen world, and they do it despite, and counterfeit it, for their own vain glory and personal gain. Think what happens when you counterfeit money. The federal government comes down hard. What does God think when you counterfeit his word, in order to turn his people into slaves? That is what these people are doing, and they are doing it in denial. They themselves are in denial of their own wicked agenda, because it is hidden in the bottom of their hearts which are deceitfully wicked, and they do not even realize that they have irreverently make the sacred vain.

That word for *vanity* is שׁוא, *shâv*, and it means; to bring desolating evil and destruction, to bring literal ruin and to be morally guile; to be filled with idolatry, and to be utterly useless, and deceptively vain, to engage in falsehood, and to lie so as to become utterly vain. The false prophets make the people vain, they desolate the people, destroying them and then they utterly ruin the church. The desolation is a barren wasteland, a dry and waterless place, where long ago the Holy Spirit has been quenched and has left, and in his place, the lying divination spirits have come in along with Angels of light bearing doctrines of demons in their hand. The word for *desolation* also means; emotionally intense grief, sadness and loneliness. The false prophets have utterly ruined the church.

This is what the false prophets have brought; profanity, pollution, vanity, desolation, and destruction, division and ultimately death. That is why the Lord has said, "I am against you, and I am against your pillows. I am against you snaring my people with false words where you hunt souls, so I am going to tear them from your hand, and the veils that you made, I will tear them from your arms and take them out of your hands and I will let my people go and I will set them free." The false prophets have taken the people into a form of slavery, a type of spiritual slavery pictured by the slavery of the Israelites in Babylon itself.

Because with your lies, you have made the heart of the righteous sad, for they put burdens on people that were not from the Lord, and these burdens were not even from God. And God said, "I did not make the heart of the righteous sad", for the Lord was not putting these burdens on the people, but the false prophets did. And they also strengthen the hand of the wicked, who would come into God's house, and the false prophets promised the wicked life so that they would not return from their wicked ways. The false prophets actually told the wicked "be blessed", and so they harden them in their sin.

This is astonishing because it is so systemic through the entire charismatic church. This is everywhere! The Scripture says, "do not say what you will do on a future date, for that is sin, rather we are to say, if the Lord wills, then we shall go." But the false prophets, and the people that operate in this divination spirit, they love to make declarations about you. I call these words, "the declarations of darkness." The people that are under this divination spirit, they do not realize a demon is speaking through them intermittently, and I have seen how this works. They are also a victim, for some of the people are actually saved Christians who have been captured by this deception, and taken by the evil one, though at some point, the Lord will have to pull them out of the lie, but at the moment they are still the victim and captive, to the deceiving spirits within.

I NEVER SAID THAT

Their human personality can be in the forefront, and they can be sweet and godly, and they know their Bible and they love Jesus, but then something will come up, and the divination spirit will come forward, and it will make a declaration of darkness, and they will say something like, "you will always struggle with this." And when this happens, you can stop them, and say, "Why would you make that declaration. Does God reveal my destiny to you? Why are you declaring my destiny?" You go back to the person and you say, "why did you say that" and then you quote exactly what they said a moment earlier, when the spirit of divination manifested, and if the human personality comes back to the forefront, the person will say to you, "I never said that."

They will not even recall the words they spoke to you. It is as if the demon ran a translation program in their mind. Now you can get into an argument between the victim and the demon, but that is pointless. You might guess that the person is lying, and I have had this pointless argument more than once with people under these divination spirits, but now I am of the opinion when the person tells you, "I never said that" though you just heard it come right out of their mouth, they are actually telling you the truth. They did not say it, but it did come out of their mouth, so this is prima facie evidence that these words came from the spirit of hell speaking through them. When you find someone who periodically speaks right out of hell, you should probably lose their phone number, and then put them on your prayer list. It is better to not speak to them again, until they have been delivered.

What is apparently happening is, in their heart they think one thing, while a demon speaks an altogether different word out of their mouth. That is why if you ask them, "why did you say this?" They immediately deny saying what you heard; and they can pass a lie detector test, because the truth is, they did not say those words, an evil spirit did.

That is the most dangerous part, because if your friends have the spirit of Jezebel operating in them, most of the time you are dealing with the human personality, but you will never know when the demon is going to come forward, and when it happens, that divination spirit is ready to guide you right into the abyss. These lying spirits will come forward, and they will start speaking, for these people hear a voice within them, and they will tell you, "I heard a voice speak to me." The spirit of divination can be strikingly accurate as to the facts of the matter at hand, it may even seem as if it was the Lord, and the false words of the lying spirits can even be confirmed by the many people operating under the same spirit of delusion, but it nevertheless came right out of hell. If you follow this divination spirit's advice, you will find yourself on the road to ruin as well.

The other thing I find with these people is that they want to cleave unto you, particularly people who have a legitimate ministry in this hour, people that are actually hearing from the

Lord and are being used by the Lord. Daniel chapter 11 talks about the men of wisdom who would come, and give insight to the many, and then it says, "many shall cleave to them with flatteries and hypocrisy." Cleaving is like a man cleaving to his wife, it is a yoking together, for they want to be more than just friends, they want more than just fellowship together, they want to sew their dress to your shirtsleeve. They want to put you in their yoke, and then they are going to want to lead. I have even had people tell me, "it's my ministry now too" talking about what God has expressly called me to do in the kingdom. I have actually had people come up to me and tell me it is their ministry now also. If it is your ministry, maybe God should just send you, and I will go do something else.

This is absolutely insane. The point I am trying to make is this, in the so called prophetic movement, which has overrun most of the charismatic church, some of you may have come out of it already and some of you may still be in it, but the vast majority what is going on, is absolute chaos and confusion, from spirits of divination. I would even argue, it is a type and a shadow of the abomination of desolation sitting in the holy place, being lifted up in the lives of the people as a counterfeit word of God.

Think about it, if in the house of Almighty God, a demon from hell is standing up and prophesying to the people, that is an abomination. And if the people listen to the demon for very long, you will find out it brought nothing but desolation. So one of the fulfillments of the prophecy of the coming of the abomination of desolation, standing in the holy place, is the false prophets operating under spirits of divination and a Kundalini anointing, the entire Satanic carnival coming into the house of God before it manifests itself before the whole earth through the words and the deeds of the false prophet who will serve the beast. It has already manifested in the church. And this abomination makes everything desolate. So my advice to you is to do as I did, and run from it. Get as far away from these people as you can.

PLAYING WITH SILLY PUTTY

I am talking about the friends you know at church who, when you pray with them, get an idea that flashes through their mind, and they tell you it is from the Lord. They will make declarations over your life, with such subtle deception, and they mean well, but they are projecting out of their own mind. I know several people that are caught up in the false prophetic movement, in spite of my patient attempts to deliver them, they simply do not want to hear it. And so, they are caught up in this new, so-called revelation, caught up in the third wave, and they flock to the churches overrun with this deception, where this is rampant. One of them had a dream, and he called me and asked me for the interpretation of it. They dreamt they were playing baseball, and all of the guys were there, and they were doing really well. They were hitting the ball, except none of the scoring counted. So, they did not have any runs on the board. It was all for nothing. Then they discovered the ball they were playing with was not a baseball at all, rather it was a big wad of silly putty. So they threw the silly putty back to the dugout and asked for a real baseball but all they got was more silly putty. That is all it had in the stadium, for there were no real baseballs. They thought they were playing baseball, but if you are playing a game you think is baseball, but you do not actually have a baseball, what game are you playing? Silly ball?

They were playing a game they called prophecy, but they do not have any true prophecy. So what are they playing? Divination. When I was a small child, I loved my silly putty. You can flatten it out, and it would pull off a perfect image of whatever it touched. Even the colors were right. It was a really good copy. And that is exactly how the false prophets operate. Whenever they touch something, whatever impression they get, they run with it, and they speak out of their religious dogma, or a divination spirit takes over and really yokes you up. And all the time they think they are speaking the truth, but they are just speaking out of their own mind, or worse.

WOMEN SHALL RULE OVER THEM

> *As for my people, children are their oppressors, and women rule over them. O my people, they which lead thee cause thee to err, and destroy the way of thy paths. The LORD stands up to plead, and stands to judge the people. Isaiah 3:12*

The Scriptures declare at the time of the end, children would become oppressors and women would rule over the church. And in their leadership, they would lead the people into error, destroying the way of their paths. And in this time, the Lord will stand up to judge the people.

The Scripture tells us to sanctify the Lord and let him alone become your fear. When you realize how systemic this satanic deception is, within both the world and the church, you will learn the fear of the Lord is the only antidote. The fear of the Lord will stop you from presumptuous sin. The fear of the Lord will become your dread, and then, the Lord will become your sanctuary. But for those who want to go on in their presumption, in their simpleminded ways, for the simpleminded believe every word, and you still want to go play that word prophecy game, you are going to find a stone of stumbling and you will find yourself falling and broken, and you might even find yourself snared and taken.

THUS SAITH THE LORD

I knew a man many years ago, who was in a leadership position, and who regularly in the course of a conversation would declare, "thus saith the Lord" quoting some Bible verse, which had passed through his understanding in the course of the conversation. Rather than sharing his insight, or opinion, he would declare it to be the word of the Lord as the conclusion of the matter being discussed. Until one day the Lord spoke to him through an angel from heaven and said, "Do not say thus saith the Lord, when the Lord has not spoken."

This man falsely believed that whatever came into his mind was somehow magically the voice of the Lord. Brethren, we have our own brains, and we have our own thoughts, and the enemy can speak things to us, and yes, the Lord can as well at times. But it is the height of folly to presume that something came from the Lord just because it flashes in your brain. It would be like taking your Bible and flipping open the pages, and assuming every time you did this, you would get a specific word from God. Now I know there are times in all of our lives, when we open the word and read something that is exactly what we need to hear. The Lord does speak like that on occasion, but not every time you open the Bible.

The true word of prophecy is a confirmation of what God has already given you in terms of direction. God is not going to send a prophet to you to tell you something he has not already impressed on your spirit. The Scriptures tell us in Micah 7, "Place no confidence in a guide, and trust not in friend." Do not look to another person as a guide. So, the Lord would not send you guidance through another person, after he just got done telling you do not go there. He sends the prophets for confirmation, and the true prophet will come to expose your sin.

THE TRUE WORD OF KNOWLEDGE

As far as the word of knowledge is concerned, a true word of knowledge will be an actual word of knowledge. Knowledge is familiarity with actual facts and information, like when Jesus was speaking to the woman at the well and he told her she had five previous husbands. The word of knowledge is not a riddle or a picture requiring interpretation. I have been around the prophetic movement for a long time, and I am glad to be out of it. I used to hear these words coming out people, which I call prophetic riddles. "I see balloons all around you." What are you supposed to do with that? "I see a dog trying to steal your keys." One woman stood up in church and declared, "I saw Jesus, like the lion of Judah and he walked into the church, and he put his paw on everybody's shoulder, he began to lick everyone." Our God is not a cartoon character, and if the Lord did come into that church as the Lion of Judah, he might give everyone a real licking, but it would be the kind where you would be smoking when it was over. Because you would be licked by the fire of his righteous judgment. What has been going on in these charasmagic churches in this hour is absolute insanity.

The worst part is much of what passes for modern prophetic words is nothing more than Christians laying yokes upon each other. This whole prophetic model is a sham; the whole concept of seeking to hear from God by looking to another man is a sham. The Lord has called for a famine of his word in the land, and he also warned us many false prophets would come in this hour. But what are the people doing, in the midst of this famine? They are running to and fro, trying to find the word of God from some man. You are only going to find the word of God when you humble yourself, shut the door of your prayer closet, begin fasting and praying, and begin seeking him with your whole heart. You are going to find the word of God when you wait on the Lord, not when you turn to hear from another man.

If you humble yourself, then maybe the Lord might speak to you in the midst of this famine. But if you look to the spirits, or if you turn to the dead, for much of the pandemonium that is occurring within the charismatic churches, is from the spirits of the dead; if you look there for knowledge, or for direction, you are going to be in real trouble. You may even find yourself doomed before time plays out, because you have literally turned to spirits of darkness for the direction in your life. And what path do you think they will counsel you on. The true prophet is going to give a true word, it will be confirmed, and then it will come to pass. The Lord wants to speak to each of us, through his word, and in his presence, through prayer. We need to slow down our busy lives and devote more time to seeking the Lord for ourselves, and stop listening to the many voices muttering all around us.

THE TRUE WORD OF PROPHECY

We are heading into a tumultuous time and we are going to need to hear what the Lord would say to us. Yes, there is a true word of prophecy. There are two prophets, who will operate in the true office of a prophet, and they are coming at the time of the end. There is the gift of prophecy, which is one of the gifts of the Holy Spirit. The New Testament tells us the gift of prophecy is for the edification of the saints, not for burdening them.

The false prophets, ultimately, want control. The true prophets do not want control you. A true prophet can give you a specific word without knowing anything about you. That is why King Nebuchadnezzar told Daniel and the rest of the wise men in Babylon, you tell me the dream and the interpretation and then I will know you are for real. The central character of the false prophet is the desire to assume authority which God has not given them, which is the essence of the satanic. The whole charismatic model is out of order, because it conditions people to look for prophetic words from men, and not to go to the Lord themselves. A generation of people get in their cars and drive around trying to find a word from the Lord, but there is no word coming. At least not that way. God does not put my mail in your mailbox.

If you look at the true prophets in the Scriptures, how much personal prophecy did any of them ever give anyone? They may have given a prophecy to the King, but that was a word to the nation or to the government. How many times did a true prophet of God give a prophecy to an individual? Almost never. We are in a time when the word of God is very precious, and we should not be running around trying to hear the word of the Lord for our brothers and sisters.

MY SHEEP HEAR MY VOICE

Jesus said, "My sheep hear my voice, and they will not follow another." Where in the Scripture are we told the sheep should turn to the other sheep to hear from the Lord? That whole model is flawed. And second, we should not be speaking all these declarations over the lives of each other as if we have the authority. The Bible says we are not even supposed to declare that were going to have lunch tomorrow. We are supposed to say, if the Lord wills. This is a major, out of order situation.

The Lord told us, "You will give an account for every word you speak" and that was for every idle word. What kind of accounting are you going to have to give for prophesying falsely in his name? The Scripture reveals that the people who prophesy falsely in his name are deleted from the writings of Israel. What if that includes the Book of Life? How many people would be quick to utter prophetic declarations if all they had to do was be wrong one time and then they would be headed to hell for eternity? The false prophets today speak their lies with impunity. They say whatever they want and they never face any consequences. The day of consequences is about to come upon us. This is a very serious sin against the body of Christ and against the Lord, to take the holy word of God and desecrate it with lies. This is no joke, for this is a deadly serious issue.

The false prophets have such an exalted opinion of themselves, and such an inflated ego, that they will proclaim whatever thought passes through their mind, assuming it to be God's word. We were warned that many false prophets would come; nowhere in Scripture does it tell us that many true prophets would come in this last hour. We are told rather, there would be a famine of hearing the true word of God in the land. We were also told, a strong delusion would come upon the church. I submit to you that the charismatic movement is under the great delusion and that spirits of divination have come in, and completely taken control. They have corrupted virtually everything that passes for a prophetic word of knowledge, and almost all of it is false. Yes, there is a real remnant that has come out of this deception, but for the most part this stuff is false and damning.

This is all just a Christian form of witchcraft, where people bind you up under their words, and they do not even know they are operating in the demonic. The Scripture declares, "If any man speaks let him speak as in Oracle of God." That word *oracle* means an infallible authority, perfect in every way. That pretty much disqualifies virtually everything being said in the church today.

Recent scientific research has discovered that the frontal lobe of the brain is the place where you can hear the Lord and the part of our mind in which we have faith. They have also discovered that all the stimulants, caffeine, nicotine, drugs, the processed foods with substances such as high fructose corn syrup, are actually creating a chemical fog in the frontal lobe of your mind making it hard for you to hear from the Lord. So, when the Lord is calling us to fasting and prayer, and even to the Daniel fast which is a vegetarian based diet, the Lord is actually calling us to detox our minds, so that we can learn to hear from him again. These long-term fasts actually clear our minds to better hear from the Lord.

The damage from all these chemicals is having a profound effect on our ability to hear and understand the things of God. And all the while the false prophets have been wasting your time at best or bringing confusion upon you and damage to you at worst. But they are not helping at all to prepare you for what is ahead of us. Turn them off. If God wants to send a prophet to you, he is able. The Lord can send somebody to your front door. You do not have to seek them out. Seek the Lord.

When you get a prophetic word from somebody, how do you confirm it? The charismatic model of everyone speaking prophetic words to each other is a deception. That is not how the early church worked. In the book of acts, they did not do what is being done in these charismatic churches in America today. This thing is an abomination, and there are people that come out of the charismatic church, but still have the spirit within them. And it is not the Lord, and look how far we have fallen.

I was born again in the charismatic movement, and I watched as it turned satanic. I tried to stand against it, but nobody wanted to listen. I have literally heard thousands of these prophetic words, given to me and everybody else. The charismatic church was not a New Age counterfeit in 1971. It was full of the Holy Spirit. This whole movement has turned into only confusion. When the church should have been diligently fasting and praying and seeking God, and humbling themselves, instead it turned into a counterfeit. False prophets might have been entertaining themselves, or thinking that this was just a sport, or they thought they had the right to rule because they were more important than everyone else. Whatever their motivation, they have done a great amount of damage to the body of Christ. The Lord says so himself, in saying, "I am against you." You have to do something seriously wrong for God to say, "I am against you. I am deleting you from all of my books in Israel."

The church has fallen into pretense. The people all pretend and then call their pretense faith. The Scripture says, "These signs will follow those who believe, in my name they will lay hands on the sick and they shall recover." In the modern church, they cannot do any of that, but there is one thing they can do, and they do it all the time, they can prophesy. They love to speak their words of knowledge, and they love to make their declarations.

If the true believers are to be healing the sick, then who is this group that all they do is speak false prophecy? Who are they? If the true Christians are casting out of devils and healing the sick, who are the people who are walking in falsehood? They are the apostasy which was prophesied to come. This is a terrifying time in human history. We would all be well advised to diligently seek the Lord. And if you have not tried praying and fasting, you should definitely put it on your calendar. It is not as hard as you think. Jesus went to the cross for us and all he asked us to do was to fast and pray a little. I think we got the easier job.

There is only one problem with fasting and praying, in order to do it, you have to do it. I had a dream in which I was flying on an airplane, and I fell asleep before the plane took off. I awoke and the plane was flying 10 miles an hour, about 10 feet off the ground. And I turned and asked the people, "Why are we flying so slow and so low." They told me, "There is no food on this airplane and we all want to eat, so we have to fly this slow to go to the next airport in the city." I responded saying, "Can't we forget the food because I want to go fast." So there you have it. If you want move forward in the kingdom of God, and fly at 40,000 feet, moving forward at 600 miles an hour, then you have to skip the airplane food and learn to fast and pray. That is the difference with prayer and fasting. If you fast and pray, you are going to move forward at 600 miles an hour, and you can fly at 40,000 feet. If you don't, you will move forward at 10 miles an hour, flying only 10 feet off the ground.

In the book of Zechariah, the prophet reveals, the curse will go forth and all the earth, in which everyone who steals, and everyone who bears false witness will be cursed.

> *"Then said he unto me, This is the curse that goes forth over the face of the whole earth: for every one that steals shall be cut off as on this side according to it; and every one that swears shall be cut off as on that side according to it." Zechariah 5:3*

The Lord testifies that this curse will "enter into the house of the thief, and into the house of him that swears falsely by my name: and it shall remain in the midst of his house, and shall consume it with the timber thereof and the stones thereof." [46] and the curse comes forth upon all those who swear falsely by my name says the Lord. Everyone who bears false witness in the name of the Lord, and everyone who steals, they shall come under the curse. Zechariah is then shown a picture of how the curse will manifest.

THIS IS THE RESEMBLANCE OF THE CURSE

Then the angel that talked with me went forth, and said unto me, Lift up now thine eyes, and see what is this that goes forth. And I said, What is it? And he said, This is an ephah that goes forth. He said moreover, This is their resemblance through all the earth. Zechariah 5:5-6

The curse is pictured coming forth as an *ephah,* which is defined as a full measure used in commerce.[47] This is the full measure of the curse, and it comes forth in terms used in commerce or business. The prophecy reveals to us this is the resemblance of the curse throughout all of the earth. The word for resemblance used in this text is עין, *ayin, ah'-yin,* which means the eye; by analogy the outward appearance, the countenance. This is what the curse looks like as it manifests in the earth. *This is their resemblance,* the resemblance of the curse. The ephah represents a full measure of the curse poured out, the unrighteous filling up the measure of their iniquity, these are they that are *meted* to destruction, as an ephah of corn measured at the market or at the mill. Some think that the mentioning of an ephah, which is used in buying and selling, intimates the fraud, deceit, and extortion often found in the commerce of this world.

"He sees a *woman sitting in the midst of the ephah,* representing the sinful church. The angel says of the woman in the *ephah, This is wickedness;* it is a wicked nation, else God would not have rejected it thus; it is as wicked as *wickedness* itself, it is abominably wicked. *How has the gold become dim! Israel was holiness to the Lord* (Jeremiah 2:3); but now *this is wickedness,* and wickedness nowhere else so scandalous, or so outrageous, as when it is found masquerading as righteousness among professors of religion. He sees the woman thrust down into the ephah, and a *talent,* or large weight, *of lead,* cast upon the *mouth* of it, by which she is secured, and made prisoner in the *ephah,* and utterly unable to get out of it."[48]

IN THE LAND OF SHINAR

He sees the ephah, with a woman thus pressed to death in it, carried away into a far country, to the land of Shinar, carried away to Babylon in captivity. The instruments employed were *women,* who had *wings like* those *of a stork,* an unclean bird; the wings are the power of the spirit, and this spirit is unclean. They *lifted it up between the earth and the heaven,* which is a picture of the mountains, or the high places, and the word used is *Oros,* which represents the nicholatin doctrines, where the pastor or priest assumes the position of ruler over the people, a people who were meant to be a nation of priests and kings themselves, who now have become slaves to their sin, and then to the false church...

> *And, behold, there was lifted up a talent of lead: and this is a woman that sitteth in the midst of the ephah. And he said, This is* ***wickedness.*** *And he cast it into the midst of the ephah; and he cast the weight of lead upon the mouth thereof. Zechariah 5:7*

WITH THE WINGS OF A STORK

This is a picture of what the wickedness of this curse of lying and stealing in the name of God would look like in the earth.

"Then lifted I up mine eyes, and looked, and, behold, there came out two women, and the wind was in their wings; for they had wings like the wings of a stork: and they lifted up the ephah between the earth and the heaven." The power lifting up this woman is pictured as two women with the wings of a stork, which are unclean birds. This represents the unclean spirits behind the manifestation of this curse. And this house was built in Shinar, which are the plains of Babylon.

> *Then said I to the angel that talked with me, whither do these bear the ephah? And he said unto me, To build it an house in the land of Shinar: and it shall be established, and set there upon her own base. Zechariah 5:10*

The process of restoration is not an easy one, nor is it a walk that many will understand. But it is a walk that is necessary if we are to return to the presence of the Father. The prophet Isaiah wrote of our day when he proclaimed:

> *But this is a people robbed and spoiled; they are all of them snared in holes, and they are hid in prison houses: they are for a prey, and none delivereth; for a spoil and none saith Restore. Isaiah 42:22 For there shall arise false Christs, and false prophets, and shall shew great signs and wonders; insomuch that, if it were possible, they shall deceive the very elect. Behold, I have told you before. Matthew 24:24-25*

The word used for false is *pseudēs*, and it means: *untrue, erroneous, deceitful, wicked:* false, liar. And the word used for deceive is *plan-ah'-o, which means* to go astray, deceive, err, seduce, wander, be out of the way.

THE DECEIVERS HAVE COME AMONG US

The deceivers have come among us, and the pastors and leaders, who were supposed to protect the sheep from this evil, were either fast asleep, or part of the deception sent by hell itself. In either event, the doors to the American church were opened wide, and a flood of deception from the mouth of the dragon has come in. We have sown to the wind, and now we shall reap the whirlwind.

> *For the time will come when they will not endure sound doctrine; but after their own lusts shall they heap to themselves teachers, having itching ears; And they shall turn away their ears from the truth, and shall be turned unto fables. 2nd Timothy 4:3-4*

> *And to you who are troubled rest with us, for the Lord Jesus shall be revealed from heaven with his mighty angels, In flaming fire taking vengeance on them that know not God, and that obey not the gospel of our Lord Jesus Christ: Who shall be punished with everlasting destruction from the presence of the Lord, and from the glory of his power; When he shall come to be glorified in his saints, and to be admired in all them that believe. 2nd Thessalonians 4:1-7*

> *Let no man deceive you by any means: for that day shall not come, except there shall come a falling away first. 2nd Thessalonians 2:3*

> *Beloved, believe not every spirit, but try the spirits whether they are of God: because many false prophets are gone out into the world. 1st John 4:1*

STRANGE FIRE

"What would God say about those who blatantly misrepresent his Holy Spirit? Who replace the biblical gospel with vain illusions of health and wealth? Who claim to prophesy in his name yet speak errors and who sell false hope to desperate people for millions of dollars? From the Word of Faith to the New Apostolic Reformation, the Charismatic Movement is being consumed by the empty promises of the prosperity gospel. Charismatic celebrities promote a form of Christianity without Christ and a Holy Spirit without holiness. And their teaching is having a disastrous influence on a grand scale as large television networks broadcast their heresies to every part of the world in strange fire."[49]

The modern charismatic movement has truly become a *Charasmagic* movement, where the many that have remained within it are now being deceived by doctrines of demons; they are bound in spiritual chains and have become slaves to the spirit of Jezebel. Unwittingly, they have now become servants of the beast. The Jesus Movement of the early 1970's witnessed powerful moves by the real Holy Spirit of God, but it was not long before the counterfeit swept in, first in the form of false worship, and then the false prophets appeared. Finally, a false anointing was poured out upon the many who no longer obey the Lord, but who only call upon his name.

Today, the world-wide charasmagic movement is full of false doctrine, and it is led by false leadership. It has literally given birth to a false church. It is now a false form of Christianity at its worst. If you look at the *Charasmagic* movement globally, aside from a remnant whom the Lord is calling out from among them, what you find is a false church ruled by false leadership following after doctrines of devils and walking under the false fire of an anti-Christ spirit of rebellion, a Kundalini anointing right out of hell, and for the most part, it is ruled by women.

In the time of Elijah, a drought was poured out as judgment upon a people who had turned from the worship of the true God of Israel unto the worship of a strange god, whom they called Ba'al. The name *Ba'al* meant Lord, and the people falsely believed they were still worshiping the true Lord, but the drought in the natural was accompanied by a drought in the spirit, and the Lord they worshipped, who they called Ba'al, was not the Lord GOD Jehovah of Israel.

Ours is also a dry land now. There is little rain falling in the natural and virtually no rain in the spirit. And the *Charismagic* movement has now become the church from Shinar, in the plains of Babylon. Like that woman Jezebel, it has been transformed into a habitation of darkness, and the people whose hearts could not discern the counterfeit from the real, have become slaves to this lying spirit.

This is where the two witnesses shall come in, for they are the sons of God, who will be full of the Oil of the true Holy Spirit. In the Temple of the Lord standing before the Throne of the Great King, is a brazen brass altar of judgment; on this altar, the red heifer is cremated, and it is from the ashes of the red heifer, mixed with water and hyssop, that true healing begins. The two witnesses will come forth from this altar, and they shall level the mountains of this false church from Babylon.

Proverbs 30

I am more brutish than any man. I have neither learned wisdom, nor have I the knowledge of the holy. Proverbs 30:2

Everyman in his own flesh is a *brute*, and the mind of a *brute* cannot receive the knowledge of the holy things of God, for the mind of the flesh has been forever corrupted by its knowledge of good and evil. This knowledge has come within the heart of every man through the fall, in which the heart of man has become utterly corrupted, and has become the heart of the *bruit.*

No matter how civil a man may appear, he remains corrupted, for by his very nature, he will always chose to remain in the dry and waterless places which are covered by the darkness of sin. Within that darkness, the heart of man hides his true nature within, and only those who have come to the place of repentance from the dead works of the flesh are able to perceive the true power of sin, for the heart of a man is so deceitfully wicked, that no man in the flesh can received the true knowledge of the holy things of God.

The true extent of the deception of mankind is only revealed by the Lord, to those who have already passed from death to life, for Jesus told us, "you shall know the truth, and the truth shall make you free."[50] Only those who have been born again can receive the knowledge of the truth, for unto everyone else, only the lie is known. The mind of flesh lives within the lie, and although it chooses to call its lies the truth, they will always remain a lie.

The word for *make you free* is *el-yoo-ther-o'-o* and it means, to liberate from mortal liability, to deliver you and to set you free. Until the truth of God's word is received within the heart of man, we cannot be free from the deceitfulness of our sin, which lies deep within the heart of every one of us. And the truth of God's word can only be known through the knowledge of Jesus Christ as the living word of God, for only the living word of God can bring true life within us. Otherwise we will remain dead in our sins, and the deception of sin will continue to remain hidden deep within the heart.

TRUST NOT IN LYING WORDS

The scripture warns us, "trust not in lying words"[51] for the mind of the flesh naturally trusts in its own lies. It believes them, for it lies to itself, before it ever lies to you. And in turning from the truth to lies, which is the nature of the mind of man, man naturally deceives himself. This is why the many on that day will cry out, "Lord, Lord", and they will be astonished when they are told, "I never knew you." In truth, the many who never knew the Lord, believed they knew him, but their faith was false, and they will discover in the end that they only believed in their own lies. Only the Lord can redeem our souls from the power of this deception within, and this redemption only operates within us when we walk in the spirit of God.

The deceptive nature of the flesh remains alive within each one of us, and if we continue to respond in the flesh, we will remain in the kingdom of lies. It is within these lies, the evil one takes away the daily sacrifice commanded us of God, and in its place, seeks to erect the abomination that makes everything desolate in the heart of a man. This abomination is the worship of idols in the holy place of our hearts, where we should worship the Lord alone. In the heart of the flesh, men worship and lift themselves up in their own eyes, full of the spirit of pride. In this deception of sin, men presume themselves to be something they are not, while they serve themselves, only pretending to serve the Lord. These are the high places erected within the minds of men, where the darkness deceives the hearts of men.

> *And he shall take away the daily sacrifice, and shall place the abomination that makes desolate. And those who do wickedly against the covenant shall he corrupt by flatteries: but the people who know their God shall be strong and do exploits. And they that understand among the people shall instruct many: yet they shall fall by the sword, and by flame, by captivity, and by spoil, many days. And when they shall fall, they shall be helped with a little help: but many shall cleave to them with flatteries.* *Daniel 11:31-34*

They that do wickedness against the covenant are corrupted by flatteries, or blandishment. The word in the text is בַּחֲלַקּוֹת *be-kal-ak-kaw-ti* and it means, to be flattered with the underlying intention of deceiving and persuading you to do something you would otherwise not choose to do. The noun *blandishment* is related to the old-fashioned verb *blandish* meaning, to coax with flattery, or kind words. As opposed to real praise, flattery is insincere and almost always has an ulterior motive. The Old English word for *flatter* originally meant, to stroke with the hand or caress, as when you stroke someone's ego to get what you want, or to gain an advantage over them.

The Hebrew notion of flattery[52] reveals these men have now become as the heathen,[53] for the word of God is no longer found as the guiding light within them anymore, and all that remains of their faith is the vain outward pretenses of a religion of men. In their hearts, the work of the deceiver has come to the full, so that the only truth which proceeds out of their mouths is the asp and the bite of the serpent within.

The men of wisdom shall be surrounded by a great company, who will claim to come to provide help; but the "little help" they provide will prove to be uttery vain, for the many who come, seeking to cleave unto them, shall do so with only flatteries, for they shall be pretend friends. Hoping to gain some advantage, they will attempt to cleave unto the men of wisdom; some will seek material gain, while others will come seeking the oil, their own lamps having none, desiring to obtain a portion for themselves from the anointed ones.

They will want to join them, or cleave unto them, and the word is עֲלֵיהֶם, from the root word לוה, *lahav* which means, to be entwined or united, to remain among them, as a borrower. And the friendship they offer is but a form of obligation, to cause them to lend. They seek to join with the men of wisdom as a borrower would join with a lender. The help which they provide is only a "little help" and it comes with a price, for the flatterers come as pretend friends, and they only come to gain some advantage for themselves.

> *Oh that I had in the wilderness a lodging place of wayfaring men; that I might leave my people, and go from them! For they be all adulterers, an assembly of treacherous men. And they bend their tongues like their bow for lies: but they are not valiant for the truth upon the earth; for they proceed from evil to evil, and they know not me, saith the LORD. Take ye heed every one of his neighbor, and trust ye not in any brother: for every brother will utterly supplant, and every neighbor will walk with slanders. Jeremiah 9:2-4*

The prophet Jeremiah wished he could hide himself in the wilderness from the faces of his people, for they were all treacherous men, who only bent their tongues for lying, and were never valiant for the truth. The works and deeds they do, in truth, proceed only from evil to evil, and they know it not. They also know not the Lord, therefore, the Lord warns the men of God, take heed of every neighbor, and all of your brothers, and trust not in any of them, for every one of them will utterly supplant, and everyone will walk with slanderers in this hour.

Matthew Henry writes of this time saying, "Go into their solemn meetings for the exercises of religion, for the administration of justice, or for commerce - to church, to court, or to the exchange - and there you find only *an assembly of treacherous men.* There they will cheat you deliberately and industriously, with design, with a malicious design, for *they bend their tongues, like their bow, for lies,* with a great deal of craft; their tongues are fitted for lying, as a bow that is bent is for shooting, and are as constantly used for that purpose. Go into their families, and you will find they will cheat their own brethren (*every brother will utterly supplant*); they will trip up one another's heels if they can, for they lie to seek an advantage. Jacob had his name from *supplanting;* it is the word here used; they followed him in his name, but not in his true character, *without guile.* So very false are they that you cannot *trust in a brother,* rather you must stand as much upon your guard as if you were dealing with a stranger, with a Canaanite that has *balances of deceit in his hand.* Go into their company and observe both their commerce and their conversation, and you will find there is nothing of sincerity or common honesty among them. *Nec hospes ab hospite tutus - The host and the guest are in danger from each other.* The best advice a wise man can give you is *to take heed every one of his neighbor,* and even of those who have befriended him, and who pretends friendship to him. No man thinks himself bound to be either grateful or sincere. Take them in their conversation and *every neighbor will walk with slander;* they care not what ill they say one of another, though ever so false; that way that the slander goes they will go; they will *walk with* it. Take them in their trading and bargaining, and *they will deceive everyone his neighbor,* will say anything, for their own advantage. Nay, they will lie for lying sake, to keep their tongues in use to it, for *they will not speak the truth,* but will tell a deliberate lie and laugh at it when they are done."[54]

THE MEN OF THIS AGE

The men of this age tell only lies, for they have all first lied to themselves, before they ever lie to you, and thus having deceived themselves, they feign lying words which they pretend to be true, but their words remain lies nevertheless. They make their beds in Sodom, and it is there in Sodom that they sleep in the night, and in the day they chose to dwell in Babylon, for it is there, that they find their delight. These are the perilous times of which we were warned would come at the end of time.

> *This know also, that in the last days perilous times shall come. For men shall be lovers of their own selves, covetous, boasters,* ***proud****, blasphemers, disobedient to parents, unthankful, unholy, without natural affection, trucebreakers, false accusers, incontinent,* ***fierce****, despisers of those that are good, Traitors, heady,* ***high minded****, lovers of pleasures more than lovers of God; Having a form of godliness, but denying the power thereof: from such turn away. For of this sort are they which creep into houses, and lead captive silly women laden with sins, led away with divers lusts, Ever learning, and never able to come to the knowledge of the truth. Now as Jannes and Jambres withstood Moses, so do these also resist the truth: men of corrupt minds reprobate concerning the faith. But they shall proceed no further: for their folly shall be manifest unto all as theirs also was." 2nd Timothy 3:1-9*

The scripture warned us, perilous times would come at the end of the age. The book of Proverbs contains the sayings of Solomon, which were given to teach us wisdom, and to make one wise. However, the 30th chapter of the Book of Proverbs was not written by Solomon, and rather than words of wisdom, it contains a prophecy of what would come at the end of times, which is our time.

"The words of Agur the son of Jakeh, even the prophecy: the man spake unto Ithiel, even unto Ithiel and Ucal."[55] The name Agur ben Jakeh, אגור בן יקה means a son who is a collector or a scribe. Agur ben Jakeh is attributed for publishing a collection of proverbs which are known as the *Book of Agur* or *Sayings of Agur*. In Hebrew, the text implies that it was composed in the gentile lands, in a district known as Mash, which lay somewhere between Judea and Babylon. The book contains the proverbs written for the *Mighty Ones*, or המשל, *Ha-Moshel of the Gibborim*.

The rabbinical writings interpret the name of *Agur* as, "the compiler"; the one who first gathered the maxims together. The son of *Jakeh* denotes one who spat out, or despised, from קוא, which means, to spit, and *le-Ithiel*, means the words of God. His name means, "I can transgress, *ukal,* the law against marrying many wives without fear of being misled by them."[56]

A PROPHECY OF THINGS TO COME

Interpreted from these rabbinical writings, Proverbs 30 is a prophecy of a future generation which would have no fear of transgressing the word of the Lord. There would be no fear of God in the land, or in the churches, or the synagogues, for the people in that age would despise what is good, while they resist the truth. They would turn the grace of God into a license for sin. They would be so full of themselves that they would lift themselves up in their own eyes, thinking they have done no wrong, for they all would stand in the hubris of their pride.

Hubris is the most extreme form of pride, and a pride so intoxicating that it indicates a loss of contact with reality; a state of drunken stupor, spiritually, a pride so intense, and an arrogance so outrageous, that that judgment of God is assured. These are a people so lost in their pride, so blind in their sin, that they have lost all contact with reality. They are asleep in

Sodom, while they only dream they walk on the mountains of Zion. They are servants who are disobedient to the Lord, who presume they are princes and priests ministering in his house, and presume they have been lifted up and given the authority to rule over his people.

Another of the rabbinical writers states, "Agur means, the one who is brave in the pursuit of wisdom, and the son of Jakeh signifies he who is freed from sin, from *naki*, and is now pure; for he carries *ha-massa*, the burden, or one who bore the yoke of God; *le-Ithiel*, for he who understood the signs of his times and he knows the deeds of God, for he who understands the Hebrew alphabet of God, and has insight into the mystery of the creative letters of the Hebrew alphabet and thus he is referred to as *we-Ukal* which may also be translated as, *the master*."[57]

> *The words of Agur the son of Jakeh, even the prophecy: the man spake unto Ithiel, even unto Ithiel and Ucal, Surely I am more brutish than any man, and have not the understanding of a man. I neither learned wisdom, nor have the knowledge of the holy. Proverbs 30:1-3*

The scripture reveals, the men of this time would be *brutish*, which is the word בער, *bah-ar* meaning stupid like cattle, or like a beast, or one that is foolish. They would neither have learned wisdom, nor have any knowledge of the true holy things of the Lord. The word for *wisdom* begins with the word נהי, *neh-hee* which means, lamentation, and wailing, for the word for wisdom is נהיר, *neh-hee-roo* which means illumination, wisdom or light.

The word for *wisdom* has, as its root, the word for lamentation, with one added letter, *Resh,* which is the 20th letter in the Hebrew alphabet and it means, *the beginning* or *the first part.* The Hebrew letter *Resh* reveals the "beginning of wisdom" is to learn obedience from the suffering in the flesh which produces lamentations and wailing. It is there, in the time of sorrow, that we first learn obedience and the fear of the Lord, which is the beginning of all wisdom. But the prophet is describing a generation of men who have neither suffered in the flesh, nor learned any of the true wisdom of the Holy and Sacred things of the Lord. Yet they are so wise, in their own eyes.

> *Who has ascended up into heaven, or descended? Who has gathered the wind in his fists? Who has bound the waters in a garment? Who has established all the ends of the earth? What is his name, and what is his son's name, if thou canst tell? Proverbs 30:4*

Who has ascended and been lifted up by God? And who has gathered the wind in his hand? The word for gathered is אָסַף, *aw-saf* which means, to gather or to receive, to bring, and to take up. Who has the Holy Spirit of God in their hands, and has received the fire from on high, such that their hands burn with the presence of the Holy One?

> *Every word of God is pure: he is a shield unto them that put their trust in him. Add thou not unto his words, lest he reprove thee, and thou be found a liar. Proverbs 30:5*

The true witnesses of the Lord do not add to his words, lest they be found to be liars. The false prophets and the false witnesses have added to the word of the Lord, words which come out of their own minds, from the dark counsel within the soul of man, yet they presume the words to be inspired, but they are all but liars and fools.

> *A fool also is full of words: a man cannot tell what shall be; and what shall be after him, who can tell him? The labor of the foolish wearies every one of them, because he knows not how to go to the city. Woe to thee, O land, when thy king is a child, and thy princes eat in the morning! Blessed art thou, O land, when thy king is the son of nobles, and thy princes eat in due season, for strength, and not for drunkenness! Ecclesiastes 10:14-17*

The foolish prophets are full of words, but they cannot tell what shall be, and their words are wearisome and full of only vanity, for they do not even know the way to the city of the Great King! They do not know the way, nor do they know what they are doing when they bring a word for you. "Remove them from my presence" cries the true prophet, and "take them far from me." The foolish prophets eat every morning, for they are ever breaking the fast each day. They consider not, that they should only eat in due season, rather they are always eating, and being always filled with food in the flesh, so they have also become full of themselves in the mind of the flesh. They think nothing of breaking the fast every morning, for they have no knowledge of the Holy One, or his ways, therefore they fail to eat in only the due seasons of time according to the commandment of the Lord. They are ignorant of the word of the Lord, and rather, they are only full of the words of men, as the brute is only full of the ways of foolishness.

Two things have I required of thee; deny me them not before I die: Remove far from me vanity and lies: give me neither poverty nor riches; feed me with food convenient for me: Lest I be full, and deny thee, and say, Who is the LORD? or lest I be poor, and steal, and take the name of my God in vain. Proverbs 30:7-9

"Neither fill me with food", for the food of men, when filled to the brim, quickly makes fools of all men. When a nation of people eats for pleasure, and when they are always filled within, it quickly becomes of nation that is also filled with sin.

Accuse not a servant unto his master, lest he curse thee, and thou be found guilty. Proverbs 30:10

There is a generation that curses their father, and doth not bless their mother. Proverbs 30:11

Jesus spoke of this time in quoting from the book of Micah in his discourse on the last days:

And ye shall be betrayed both by parents, and brethren, and kinsfolks, and friends; and some of you shall they cause to be put to death. And ye shall be hated of all men for my name's sake. Luke 21:16-17

The text he was quoting from is found in Micah chapter seven:

The best of them is as a brier: the most upright is sharper than a thorn hedge: the day of thy watchmen and thy visitation cometh; now shall be their perplexity. ***Trust ye not in a friend, put ye not confidence in a guide****: keep*

> *the doors of thy mouth from her that lies in thy bosom. For the son dishonors the father, the daughter raises up against her mother, the daughter in law against her mother in law; a man's enemies are the men of his own house. Therefore I will look unto the LORD; I will wait for the God of my salvation: my God will hear me. Rejoice not against me, O mine enemy: when I fall, I shall arise; when I sit in darkness, the LORD shall be a light unto me. I will bear the indignation of the LORD, because I have sinned against him, until he pleads my cause, and executes judgment for me: he will bring me forth to the light, and I shall behold his righteousness. Micah 7:4-9*

The word of God warns us to trust not in our friends, for many shall be offended in this hour, and place no confidence in any guide, for there are no guides coming among us. We must all learn to hear from the Lord now. All of those who would presuppose they are a guide sent by the Lord are but liars, and that will soon be clear for all to see.

> *Notwithstanding the land shall be desolate because of them that dwell therein, for the fruit of their doings. Feed thy people with thy rod, the flock of thine heritage, which dwell solitarily in the wood, in the midst of Carmel: let them feed in Bashan and Gilead, as in the days of old. According to the days of thy coming out of the land of Egypt will I shew unto him marvelous things. The nations shall see and be confounded at all their might: they shall lay their hand upon their mouth, their ears shall be deaf. They shall lick the dust like a serpent, they shall move out of their holes like worms of the earth: they shall be afraid of the LORD our God, and shall fear because of thee. Micah 7:13-17*

And the land shall be *desolate*, שממה, *shem-aw-maw* which means, devastation and an astonishment: to be laid most desolate, as an utter wasteland. Our land is now desolate, because of the fruit of the doings of the people of this nation, and of the church that was called by his name, so the people shall now be fed with the rod of his judgment, and they shall bear the indignation and judgment alone, in solitary places.

They shall dwell on Mount Carmel, which lies at the entrance to the Valley of Jezreel, which is the valley of the mountain of Megiddo, which in the Hebrew is called, הר מגדון, *Har Megiddo* or *Armageddon*. They will feed in Bashan, which is the place of strength, and in Gilead, as in the ancient times. The name *Gilead* means, both a memorial for eternity, and the place of everlasting joy. It is there, in the mountain of Carmel, each one of us will make the choice, which God will we serve, and which of the prophetic voices in the land will we choose to follow. The ones who choose the Lord, Jehovah, and turn away from the voices of the prophets of Ba'al, and will be led into to the valley of decision, which is Jezreel, and there the remnant will pass under the rod of judgment and having bowed down under the rod, forsaking their pride, they shall pass on to the place of strength in the Lord, which is pictured as Bashan, the strongest of trees being from Bashan, and there, being strengthened in the Lord, they shall go on to Gilead.

> *I will bring them again also out of the land of Egypt, and gather them out of Assyria; and I will bring them into the land of Gilead ... And they shall pass through the sea with affliction, and shall smite the waves in the sea, and all the*

> *deeps of the river shall dry up: and the pride of Assyria shall be brought down, and the scepter of Egypt shall depart away. And I will strengthen them in the LORD; and they shall walk up and down in his name, saith the LORD. Zechariah 10:10-12*

> *There is a generation that is pure in their own eyes, and yet is not washed from their filthiness. There is a generation, O how lofty are their eyes! And their eyelids are lifted up. There is a generation, whose teeth are as swords, and their jaw teeth as knives, to devour the poor from off the earth, and the needy from among men. Proverbs 30:12-14*

Ours is the generation which is pure in their own eyes; everyone assuming they are washed from their sin, yet the Scripture declares the people are not yet washed from their sin. This generation also has such lofty eyes, and how high are they lifted up in their pride saying, "I am priest, and I have the mind of Christ", yet they sleep in Sodom and bring the familiar spirit and the family devils for all of their holiday portraits. And their teeth are as swords, which are quick to wound.

> *The leach has two daughters, crying, Give, give. There are three things that are never satisfied, yea, four things say not, It is enough: The grave; and the barren womb; the earth that is not filled with water; and the fire that saith not, It is enough. The eye that mocks at his father, and despises to obey his mother, the ravens of the valley shall pick it out, and the young eagles shall eat it. Proverbs 30:15-17*

They have the spirit of the leach within, always looking for more, what can they take, looking only to what is for them.

> *There be three things which are too wonderful for me, yea, four which I know not: The way of an eagle in the air; the way of a serpent upon a rock; the way of a ship in the midst of the sea; and the way of a man with a maid. Proverbs 30:19*

> *Such is the way of an adulterous woman; she eateth, and wipeth her mouth, and saith, I have done no wickedness. Proverbs 30:20*

> *For three things the earth is disquieted, and for four which it cannot bear: a servant when he reigns; and a fool when he is filled with meat; or an odious woman when she is married; and an handmaid that is heir to her mistress. Proverbs 30:21-23*

The whole earth is disquieted when these servants who presume themselves kings, lift themselves up and try to reign.

> *There be four things which are little upon the earth, but they are exceeding wise: The ants are a people not strong, yet they prepare their meat in the summer; The conies are but a feeble folk, yet make they their houses in the rocks; The locusts have no king, yet go they forth all of them by bands; The spider taketh hold with her hands, and is in kings' palaces. Proverbs 30:24-28*

> *There are three things which go well, yea, four are comely in going: A lion which is strongest among beasts, and*

turns not away for any; A greyhound; and a he goat also; and a king, against whom there is no rising up. Proverbs 30:29-31

"If thou hast done foolishly in lifting up thyself, or if thou hast thought evil, lay thine hand upon thy mouth. Proverbs 30:32

Surely the churning of milk brings forth butter, and the wringing of the nose brings forth blood: so the forcing of wrath brings forth strife. Proverbs 30:33

And he said: 'Thy name shall be called no more Jacob, but Israel; for thou hast striven with God and with men, and hast prevailed.'

Woe unto you, when all men shall speak well of you! for so did their fathers to the false prophets. Luke 6:26

There was corn in the land of Egypt and the seed of corn which would be lifted up in the land of Egypt would be given a new name: ZAPHENATH-PANEAH, צָפְנַת פַּעְנֵחַ. Joseph was given a new name on the day when he was promoted by Pharaoh as ruler over all of Egypt, the super power over the entire earth in that time of antiquity. Now Joseph would now be known as ZAPHENATH-PANEAH. In the writings of Josephus we are told that this name meant, "the revealer of secrets."[58] The most widely accepted meaning of this name is, "God speaks and he lives"[59] or, "God said he will live."[60] E. Naville suggested that Zaphenath Paneah was not a name, but a title, which meant: "The head of the sacred college of magicians"[61] or, "the ruler over all the wise men of Egypt." Others describe the meaning of his name as "the one who furnishes the nourishment of life," and also "the chief steward of this realm."[62]

> *Only by pride cometh contention: but with the well advised is wisdom. Proverbs 13:10*

> *Delight is not seemly for a fool; much less for a servant to have rule over princes. Proverbs 19:10*

The word for *delight* in this text is תַּעֲנוּג, *tah-an-oog* which means, luxury, delightful or pleasant things. The word *seemly* means suitable or appropriate. It is not appropriate that a fool should have delightful, luxurious or pleasant things in his life, for the nature of their foolishness keeps these things from them. Even if they be rich, their foolish ways, like the fly which spoils the ointment or the little foxes which ruin the gardens, ultimately undo even the pleasant things in their lives, bringing them to ruin. Much less is it appropriate for a servant to rule over princes. The word used for *princes* is שַׂר, *sar* which means, a head person, a governor, master, prince or a ruler.

The wealth of this world is not given to fools, much less is the wealth of the Kingdom of God given to those who are foolish spiritually. No, the wealth of the Kingdom of God is given unto those who earn it, and who are wise in their use of it. The wealth of the Kingdom is in the hand of the Lord Jesus Christ. He alone holds the gold of the kingdom in his hand, giving it to whomever he chooses. But he does not give it to fools. Even more so, it is inappropriate for those who are servants, to presume they may exercise authority over princes. And yet this is what the false prophets do, when they presume to speak the declarations out of their own heart, which in truth, is but the heart of a fool. Anyone who presumes to speak for the Lord, when the Lord has not spoken, is by definition a fool, for only a fool would presume to speak for the Holy One.

> *The remnant of Israel shall not do iniquity, nor speak lies; neither shall a deceitful tongue be found in their mouth: for they shall feed and lie down, and none shall make them afraid. Zephaniah 3:13*

> *Melchisedec received tithes of Abraham, and blessed him that had the promises. And without all contradiction the less is blessed of the better. Hebrews 7:6-7*

Those who lift themselves up over the people shall soon be cut down as in the rebellion of Korah in the wilderness. Only those who have been appointed by the Lord himself may exercise legitimate authority over the people of God. Melchisedec was afforded the greater honor, in that it was his place and privilege to bless Abraham. Hebrews 7:7 reveals, "*the lesser is blessed of the greater.*" He who gives the blessing is greater than he who receives it; and therefore Christ, who is Melchisedec, is the merited one, for he alone is the Mediator of all blessings to the children of men, and he is greater than all the priests of the order of Aaron. All others who lift themselves up as priests over the people of God are mere usurpers, and are merely deceivers who are walking under the darkness of pride. Thinking themselves as above the people, they will one day awake to find they were merely sleeping in Sodom.

The Narrow Way

Strait is the gate, and narrow is the way, which leads unto life, and few there be that find it.
Matthew 7:14

This is an hour in which there is a famine in the land for the true word of God, and yet within the Holy Place of the Lord there remains bread for the remnant of God. A remnant is now being provided living manna from heaven, for it is only given unto those who are seeking the Lord with all of their heart. The Spirit of God is trumpeting the truth in this hour, and the *Rhema* word of God is still very much alive, but it is reserved for only a remnant of the people.

WISDOM IS JUSTIFIED BY HER CHILDREN

Wisdom is justified by her children and she is confirmed by the fruit she bears. It is vitally important that we understand the Lord in this hour, and that we are able to hear what the Spirit of God is speaking to the churches. And we must to get this right. We do not have the luxury of missing the Lord in this hour. We have to be on the same page that the Lord is on. In order to receive the living manna from heaven, we must have the wisdom of God within our hearts and the wisdom from above starts with the fear of the Lord. We need to understand and receive the fear of the Lord as he would teach it and not as men have taught. The Scripture teaches that many of the people only fear God based on the teachings of men, and that is not the fear of the Lord at all.

The Word of the Lord is a very serious issue in this hour. This is not an hour to be a hearer of the word only. This is an hour to be a doer of the word. Ours is not an hour to only listen and then forget; this is an hour where we must allow the word of God to change our hearts and our lives.

BE THOU DILIGENT IN ALL THY WAYS

In order to find the true living manna from heaven, we must seek the Lord with all of our hearts, and that takes work and determination. But we live in a society where the majority of men no longer seek the Lord by striving to enter in, rather ours is the time when many are woefully complacent about the things of God, for we live in a time of the "slothful man." The Scriptures admonish us to be diligent in all of our ways, and rebukes the complacent ones who are called "slackers" or the "slothful ones." For many, this is their spiritual condition. What the Scripture reveals in the word of God in the natural, also speaks to the spiritual man. We have a responsibility on how we handle the word of God, and how we respond to the instruction of the Lord.

If we don't respond properly, we will actually bring judgment upon our lives. The word for *slacker* in Hebrew means a slothful man, an idle man. It also translates as deceitful, and full of treachery and falsehood.

> *He becomes poor who deals with a slack hand but the hand of the diligent makes rich. Proverbs 10:4*

THE HAND OF THE SLACKER BRINGS ONLY POVERTY

The hand of the slacker will bring poverty, not only in the natural but in the spirit. This is a picture of the church today, in which many are in spiritual poverty because the church in our time is full of slackers. The last day's church is the Laodicean church; and it is a congregation full of slackers.

The hand of the slacker brings only poverty, whereas the hand of the diligent brings prosperity. The word for *diligent* means decisive, or a threshing edge with sharp teeth. The hand of those who have sharp teeth in their threshing instrument will bring prosperity. The word *diligent* also means eager and the hand of the determined, the hand of those who are sharp. The word decisive means penetrating, an acute observer.

The diligent are described as those who study the word of God accurately and in a penetrating way. Is also translates as icy, knife like reasoning, with intense focus, a sharpened mind with penetrating insight and with piercing, keen discernment; the ability to perceive clearly which is suitable for cutting and separating the clean from the unclean, and for separating truth from error; discerning the will of God from the imaginations of men, and accurately cutting, dividing while sharply focused. The diligent are capable of clear thinking, which is impressively direct. These are the attributes of the diligent.

If you have these attributes spiritually, you are going to prosper in the things of the Lord. And you are going to bring forth much fruit, but with the slacker and the slothful it is not so, for they are disinclined to work. They are disinclined to exert the effort necessary to develop the keen discernment or the effort required to engage in accurate and sharply focused thinking. That takes too much work. The slothful are defined as lazy and shiftless idle youth, who are inactive. They are the *do nothing sluggards,* and they are good for nothing, indolent, totally adverse to any effort or activity. These are the habitually lazy, lacking any effort or movement, deadbeats, idlers, loafers and slugs. To be slack is to not use due diligence, or adequate care; to lack energy and to operate on low speed, lacking completion, lacking perfection and therefore, negligent in their duties and lukewarm in their commitments. These are the slackers. They prefer to do everything as if they live on easy street. They are just taking it as it comes. They do not want to get too serious.

The most insidious part of this sinful attitude is that in this hour, this lackadaisical attitude has been misunderstood and falsely defined as faith. It is not faith, it is foolishness. The slacker will not even get up in the morning, to confront the enemy and yet he calls his lazy behavior faith. The slacker will say, "Well, I am just trusting the Lord." No, the slackers do not trust the Lord; they are just lazy or incompetent. The David's that are going forth to confront the Giants are the diligent and they are the ones who are trusting the Lord because they may not be coming back alive without the intervention of the Lord. But the slackers, they stay home, for they are afraid to even venture out of the house for there may be a lion in the road.

The slothful man saith, there is a lion in the way.
Proverbs 26:13

To the diligent belongs the kingdom, and to the slacker belongs the condemnation of the King.

See thou a man diligent in his business? He shall stand before kings; he shall not stand before common men. Proverbs 22:29

The diligent are those who are incisive and penetrating in their insight, and when they begin their work, they complete it, with sharp discernment, for they are clear thinking and impressively direct. They shall stand before kings, because their work and their deeds are done with perfection. The man who is diligent in the things of the God, he shall stand before the King of kings to minister on behalf of the Lord.

As vinegar to the teeth and smoke in the eyes so the slacker is to him that sends him. Proverbs 10:26

"Those that are of the slothful disposition, that love their ease, cannot apply their mind to any business. They are not fit to be employed, no, not so much as to be sent on an errand, for they will neither deliver a message with the care nor make any haste back. Those that are guilty of such great oversight to entrust any such man with any affair and put any confidence in such people will certainly have vexation of soul with them." [63]

The slacker cannot be trusted to do anything well, for he is an utterly untrustworthy man. His "yes" does not mean "yes" nor does he attend diligently to the condition of his flock. He is just taking it as it comes.

The hand of the diligent shall bear rule but the slothful shall be under tribute. Proverbs 10:24

The word in this text for *bear rule* [64] is *mashawl* משל and it means to have dominion, as a governor, to reign and have power. The hand of the diligent shall be full of the power of the Lord. But the slothful will be under tribute. The word for *tribute* means a burden, a tax, or to be under forced labor. The hand of the slothful shall be burdened under forced labor.

TO HIM WHO OVERCOMES

"To him who overcomes, they will be given the authority to sit on thrones and rule with the Lord."

In the Scripture we are told those who overcome will rule in his power. These are the diligent among us. Those who overcome are the ones diligent in following the commandments of the Lord. The slothful are not like them, for they could take it or leave it. And if it requires much work, they are going to leave it. We are going to find out that overcoming the battle that is upon us is definitely going to require some work and some serious effort and the sluggard and the slothful need not apply. That presents no problem for them, for they will not choose to apply.

But they will be under the tribute. They will not have the dominion spiritually, nor will they have the anointing, for they are the foolish virgins who are found without the oil. They did not bother to get any oil for it took too much effort. They could not be troubled with keeping their lamps full. And so they will one day be awakened to the sound of the bridegroom, but they have no oil and no light within them for they expected it to just be given to them. But it is not given, it is earned.

He that has been faithful in a few things shall be made ruler over many. If you are diligent in the small things the Lord gives you to do, and are faithful and diligent to the fullness of your ability, you will be given authority over many things. But to the slothful, theirs is the way to slavery. Those that are *careless* and the word actually translates as deceitful, because they are deceiving themselves, they will come under the rule of a harsh master. And in the spirit, they are actually under the rule of Satan. They have not driven out the enemy, and they have not kept up the wall of the hedge around their hearts, nor have they kept the covenant, for they were content to just be lax. What does it matter? Why is it that important? To them it is not. And so they do not have, and in their lack, they fall under the dominion of others.

THE CARELESS AMONG US

They are the compromised, because it takes too much effort to stand. These are the careless ones, they will not endure the pain and the agony of striving to enter by the narrow way, no; they would rather just go the easy way. In the end, you will find them on the Broadway, which is the wide road that leads to destruction. Not only will the slothful walk in poverty in the natural, all of their days, but they will walk in poverty in the spirit as well. No doubt we have all met those of this company, and they will tell you they are under a curse of poverty. No, they have cursed themselves by their disobedience to the commandments of the Lord.

Those that are diligent, and hard-working, are in reality the ones who are truthful and when they approach their ministry or their occupation or any matter, they approach it with all of their might, and all of their heart. But not so the slackers. No, they must be servants to the wise, because they themselves will never attend fully to any matter whether in the natural world or in the kingdom that is coming.

The slothful man roasts not that which he took in hunting: but the substance of a diligent man is precious. Proverbs 12:27

The slothful man looks to prepare his dinner from what someone else captured hunting. He is simply too lazy to hunt for himself, expecting others to feed him, and also in the things of the Spirit, he is too lazy to do the work necessary to break through on his own, and far too lazy to study the Scriptures as a Berean. He is too lazy to labor in fasting and prayer, for him, it is just so much easier to sit on his La-Z-Boy recliner, laying around, and turn on the TV to watch the images of Babylon and laze away his days.

The way of the slothful man is hedged with thorns, but the way of the righteous is made plain. Proverbs 15:19

The word for *slothful* in this verse is translated as indolent, or habitually lazy and it also means slow to mature, slow to develop, and adverse to any effort. The Scripture contrasts the slothful with the righteous. On the one hand, you have the righteous, and their ways are made plain, and the word *plain* [65] is *salal,* סלל and it means to exalt, to be lifted up and to be raised up. The way of the righteous is exalted, because they are walking in God's way. But the way of the wicked, which is the opposite of the righteous, is described in the Scripture as the way of the slothful. The Lord takes our labor seriously.

He that is slothful in his work is a brother to him that is a great destroyer. Proverbs 18:9

In this Scripture the word *slothful* [66] is רפה, *raphah,* and it means to slacken, to fall, to faint, to forsake, to become idle, to leave and to become slothful. He that faints in his work, and he that forsakes his work, or he that leaves his work undone, he is the brother to him that is a great destroyer. The word for destroyer means corruption and to destroy. The slothful man is the same as the destroyer. This is a serious issue.

> *The desire of the slothful man kills him, for his hands refuse to labor. Proverbs 21:25*

The desire of the slothful is to take it easy, for he is always looking for the easy way out of work. He is looking to avoid the burden given unto him from the Lord, and that desire is literally killing him. The misery of the slothful man is great for his hands refuse to labor, thus he becomes an enemy even to himself. His desire is impetuous. He covets greedily all the day long, crying, "give, give" expecting everybody to do what he should do for himself though he will do nothing for himself, much less for anybody else. Those that are slothful in the affairs of their soul, yet have desire towards that which would be the happiness of their soul, this desire kills them. It aggravates their condemnation, and in the end, is a witness against them.

They understand the value of spiritual blessings, but they refused to be subject to the pain that is necessary to receive them. In the kingdom of God, we have to do the work of the kingdom. Yes, we were saved by grace, and it was through unmerited favor that the Lord opened the door for us to enter into covenant with him. But now that we have come into the covenant, the Lord commands us to work, to labor, and to pick up our cross. The Scripture teaches us that those who believe shall cast out devils, and shall lay hands on the sick and they will recover. These signs and wonders will follow the work of the true believer, but the slothful have nothing to do in this matter.

We live in a slothful hour, for this is a slothful age. The era of socialism is an age of slothfulism. Those who are slothful in the natural, suffer the consequences in this life, whereas those that are slothful in the affairs of the spirit, suffer in both the present world and hereafter. They are bringing judgment upon themselves, which manifests both in this world and the next. The righteous, who the Scripture calls the diligent ones, they all prosper. They are the industrious ones, for they seek, and they knock. They ask and then they find, and so, their desire is satisfied. They cry out to the father, night and day, in prayer and fasting, and they diligently study the word. Their diligence is rewarded, for they seek not only their own blessing, but they stand in the gap for others. They are willing to lay their lives down for their friends and family. Whereas the slothful are only willing to receive, they are not even willing to do the work for their own blessing, let alone stand in the gap for another.

> *The slothful man saith, there is a lion without, and I shall be slain in the streets. Proverbs 22:13*

The slothful man is always full of excuses. "Brother, I can't do that. I can't fast and pray. Pray with you for an hour. I can't and I won't." The slothful man is always full of excuses.

> *I went by the field of the slothful and by the vineyard of the man void of understanding; and, lo, it was all grown over with thorns, and nettles had covered the face thereof, and the stone wall thereof was broken down. Then I saw, and*

> *considered it well: I looked upon it, and received instruction.* Proverbs 24:30-32

Our hearts and our lives are like the field or the vineyard in the proverb. If you want to find a man who is void of understanding, you will find his witness by just looking at the field that is his life and his heart. The word for *void* [67] is חסר, *chaser*, and it means lacking or destitute, failing, full of need and to have want. The man void of understanding is destitute and failing. The word for *understanding* translates as in the heart, the feelings, or of the will and the intellect, to care, or to be courageous and to be a friend, to have understanding, to be willing, and to have wisdom.

I walked by the field of those who were utterly lacking courage, and lacking in any concern for their friends, lacking any wisdom and to those who were destitute of feelings and had no heart, "and lo, it was grown over with thorns, and nettles have covered the face thereof and the stone wall thereof was broken down." I saw the desolation, and I considered it well; I looked upon it and received instruction.

> *Yet a little sleep in a little slumber a little folding of the hands to sleep, and so shall poverty come is one that travels, and thy want as an armed man.* Proverbs 24:33-34

Each of us has been appointed as stewards over the matters of our own heart, and our souls are the fields or vineyards that we must work diligently in order to tend and keep our hearts. We are capable of improving our hearts, provided we exercise good care and good husbandry. We must become good husbands of our own hearts; we must remove the stones, and we can rebuild the hedge, and it is essential that we pull the weeds out, which are the roots of bitterness, or we can ignore them and let them fall into disrepair. We have been charged to occupy, and to tend to the field of our own heart until our Lord comes. And with great care and pain, we are required to attend to the matters of our own heart. The fields and vineyards, representing the hearts in men, are often in a very bad state, not only is there no fruit coming out of these fields, but for many, their hearts are overgrown with thorns and briars. The thorns and briars represent the inordinate lust of the flesh, the pride of life, or the spirit of covetousness, and sensuality, which is the lasciviousness of this hour. Malice and bitterness are the thorns and nettles that are like wild grapes and this is the normal crop of weeds that grow in the un-sanctified heart.

Your heart is like a garden. If you plant a garden and then do not tend to the garden, and you take a slothful attitude, fold your hands for a little sleep, you will soon find that garden overrun with weeds, choking out the true crop which would have produced real fruit and all you will get is thorns.

IN THE HEARTS OF THE SLOTHFUL ONES

In the fields of the slothful, there is no guard or protection against the enemy, for the stone wall that was to be the hedge against the onslaught of the enemy is broken down and now the field and the vineyard lie exposed and opened to enemy occupation. This is a picture of the church, which in terms of the true fruit of the spirit, is for the most part, unfruitful.

The best of them is as a brier: the most upright is sharper than a thorn hedge: the day of thy watchmen and thy visitation cometh; now shall be their perplexity. Micah 7:4

The day of the watchmen is the Day of the Lord, and in this day, the Scripture declares that, "The best of them is a thorn hedge and the most upright among them is worthless."

We, as a people have watched the walls all fall to the ground, not only in our nation, but within the church and within our families for the thorns and the briars have overrun many places. We live in a generation of people that are hearers of the word only. American Christianity is a religion of hearing and learning about the Bible, but that is where it stops for the majority of the people. They are hearers only and if they do anything at all, it is to argue about the Bible with each other. They debate and argue among each other, but they do not do the works of the kingdom, for they are ever learning but never coming to the knowledge of the living truth which is Jesus.

The stone wall that has been broken down was supposed to be the hedge which protects us from the enemy. We can now see the effect of its fall, for the curse has come upon the ground in the hearts of many. And it is in with great effort that we must recover this ground, but the slothful will never recover any of it. We must be diligent; if you have ever had a garden overrun with weeds, how intensely do you have to go after that ground in order to actually get the weeds out?

I live in Idaho, where everyone has a garden, and there is a weed that has come, and it is not from this area. The locals call it the "devil weed" and it is an evil one. This weed puts roots out twenty feet sideways under the ground and it is almost impossible to eradicate once it takes root because it sows its own seeds into the ground and then chokes out everything. It wraps itself like a serpent, around all of your produce until it chokes out all of the fruit in your garden. It will kill all of your crops. This weed came onto my land, about two years ago, and I have neighbors who have the weed as well, and they said, "There is nothing we can do." So they did not try to stop it, and thus it overran their entire land and it is now covered. I don't give up so easily. I said, "I don't care what it takes, I am going to stop this weed and don't tell me it's impossible." Well it took a lot of effort; I can tell you that much. I boiled water, to pour on this weed. I dug up the roots, I hired young men to help, I did everything I could to eradicate this weed, and so, I no longer have this weed in my garden.

INTENSE COMMITMENT IS REQUIRED

Eradicating this weed did not come by a slothful attitude, it required intense commitment. That is how it is with our hearts as well. There are some intense weeds that have been sown in this last hour, and there is some intense deception that has been sown as well. We must be diligent to pull this stuff out of our lives, and the slothful simply will not.

There is a great difference between the actions and the commitment of the people that are slothful and the ones that are diligent. The difference witnesses itself in the management of their natural affairs as well as the affairs of the kingdom. The diligent do well in all things they undertake to perform. They complete them and do well, while the others by their lack of commitment proclaim their slothfulness. It manifests in everything they do. And those that pass by and look upon them will see their home in disrepair, and their gardens overrun, for the sin of slothfulness will be evident in all of the dimensions of their life.

Solomon in Proverbs, says, "I passed by the garden of the slothful man, and I looked and received instruction." The wise man will always profit far more than fools for a wise man can learn from the folly of fools. A wise man will look at the garden of a fool and say, "I don't want my garden looking like that" but the fool cannot look at the garden of the wise man and learn anything at all. The fool will look at the garden of the wise and say, "You are really fortunate that weeds don't grow in your garden" and they will call the prosperity of the wise good fortune. They will say, "God has really blessed you, but I have a spirit of poverty on my life, please pray for me brother."

ONLY FOOLING THEMSELVES

The fools in the end only fool themselves, for in the attitude of sluggard, are the ways which lead to poverty, both in this world, and the next. Those who are prospering spiritually are doing so out of their own hard labor, and that is always the truth. Paul wrote, "If a man won't work, then don't let him eat." And if a man won't work and labor in the Spirit in the things of the Kingdom, then don't let him eat the living manna which comes out of heaven. We have all seen this in the lives of people at church, and in the homes of those who are simply not responsible. They are not responsible in the natural, and they are not responsible in the spirit. These are the people that are always struggling, and finally, when they get a job, they quit after a few days. They are in desperate shape financially, but they quit. And if you asked them, "what went wrong?" They will tell you, "Oh, that job was too hard. My feet hurt, or I had to get up too early, or it required me to work too hard."

Thus, they remain in poverty. Those that have been blessed and have prospered, worked when it hurt, and they got up early, for they did whatever it takes, and the same is true in the realm of the spirit. You have one group who will tell you, "I'm sorry but I just can't fast and pray" because they will not go to that level of effort. Then you have another group that says, "I don't care what effort is required, I'm doing it, no matter what it takes. I don't care how hard it is, and I don't care what price is required, I'm going to pay it. I am not quitting, for where else would I go?" Jesus is the only one who has the words of life. There is no other option; we either follow the Lord or we perish. We either do what it takes or we do not. And when the Lord says, "jump", the diligent and the wise all say, "how high?" That is the attitude of the diligent, and they are the ones who will one day overcome. The wise will learn from the example of the fools. Solomon received instruction by the things he saw, the ridiculous folly of the slacker, who when he should be working, lays in his bed sleeping.

GOOD FOR NOTHING

The slothful ones are all dull and stupefied for they are good for nothing, and of a certainty, misery will accompany them through all of their days. Their poverty will come upon them as an armed man, and strip them of all they have. There is also a spiritual poverty that comes as well, in the form of an armed adversary. This game we call life is for real. In this hour, the game is for all of the marbles, brethren.

This is the time to put up or shut up; either show up or forget about it. There is no more time for talking. We are entering into these events, and we have to dig down deep now. If you are willing to do the work, you will prevail. This attitude of the overcomer and it applies to all dimensions of our life. Not only our worldly occupation, but our spiritual condition as well. And the slothful, it is scandalous how they behave. They are injurious, not only to themselves, but to their families as well. They do great harm, not only to their own souls but to the souls of those they are responsible for.

We live in a time where the majority of the people do not take responsibility for anything. We have a government that is built upon the promise to provide for those who are irresponsible. They call it social justice, where they take from those that are producing and give to those that are slothful. The Bible says if a man does not work, then he should not eat. The God of heaven is not a socialist. The Scriptures very clearly advocate private property ownership, and personal responsibility and accountability. There is a special class of people that the Scripture calls the poor, who are the widows and orphans, and within that class, the people are incapable of helping themselves. The Scripture is very clear that we, the people of God, are required to provide for the welfare of the widows and orphans that are among us. But that is not the case for men and women who are capable of working and providing for themselves. Those who simply do not want to work, or who do not want to work that hard.

The amount of work that you put into something is directly correlated to the amount of benefit or production that comes out the other side. If you work modestly, you will produce modestly. If you work exceptionally hard, you will reap exceptional profit, and there is no substitute. We live in a time when truth has been so twisted that even the concept of how the Lord blesses us is misunderstood.

THE CHURCH IN SHINAR IS FULL OF LIES

The false church from Shinar is full of false teachings and one of the false teachings is that, if you give your money to the false prophets and to the false teachers, then you will get the blessing a hundred fold or a thousand fold and it will just simply fall out of heaven and drop in your lap or end up in your mailbox. Well nothing could be further from the truth, for it does not really work that way at all. The way the Lord blesses a man, is by prospering him in the things he does. God blesses his business with favor and success through work of his hands; you work hard in your garden, then the Lord causes it to rain, and the sun shines on your crop and you bring forth fruit, thirty fold, sixty fold or a hundred fold.

In this twisted hour, people believe in this pyramid scheme where if you put $1,000 into the casino church in Shinar, at some point your number is going to come up and you will finally get the hundred thousand dollar jackpot. This is so obviously false, because it were true, if it really worked that way, then those evangelist flying in Learjet's would give their money to you, so they could get the hundred to one payoff. The Lord does all things according to righteousness, and if God were to simply print up a bunch of money, like our federal government does, and drop it from a helicopter like Ben Bernanke did, he would be counterfeiting and that would be unrighteous. The process which our government calls, "quantitative easing" is really a form of counterfeiting our currency, and it is actually the devaluation of all the other money in circulation owned by everyone else. Thus it is a form of theft and it is altogether unrighteous.

So the Lord is not going to engage in unrighteous means in order to bless his people; that whole concept is false, for in order for wealth to be given to you, it has to come from someone else. And if it does not come in an exchange of equal value, then someone has been injured and defrauded. The way the Lord blesses and prospers his people is that he increases the value of what that man does. So he can then exchange the value of his personal effort in the marketplace in a fair and righteous transaction with others and receive a larger and larger reward. But the pyramid scheme, which is really the way our government is run, and is also the way the church in Shinar is structured, is in fact unrighteous and not even true.

THE GREAT PYRAMID SCHEME

The entire prosperity gospel is nothing more than a pyramid scheme. Under the laws of the United States, in any other circumstance, the people selling this fraud would be guilty of a federal crime, but because the pyramid scheme is sold in the context of religion, the charlatans who sell these lies hang their hat on the concept of faith. And because the pyramid scheme involves religious faith, it is exempt from prosecution under the Ponzi scheme laws. But it is still a pyramid scheme, for the people at the top of the pyramid always take in all of the money. But they promise you, if you give them all your money, at some point, you will be moved up to the top of the pyramid, but it never does happen, because the men selling these lies, are always the ones on top. The only person that wins is the liar at the top.

I have a friend and his parents were pastors, and they were caught up in the false prosperity gospel forty years ago, when it first came out. They put in all of their money and they believed, for they had the faith. On weekends, they would take their children to look at million dollar homes and they would tell them, one day God is going to give us a house like this. Forty years later, they are still waiting, and now they are buying lottery tickets, but gambling is not scriptural, and it is not of the Lord. God does not use the lottery to bless his people. The Scripture actually says, "riches won hastily are a curse." And forty years later, they are still living in poverty, and they have been in poverty for all this time. Now they are living with one of their children in a two-bedroom apartment, and they live in absolute poverty. They have lived in poverty their entire lives for they have believed in a scam. The Lord does not prosper you based upon deception nor does being slothful bring a blessing. You cannot be slothful or lackadaisical in life, or in the kingdom, and then prosper. We must become diligent and hardworking if we want to prosper spiritually.

You must become diligent, if you want the reward of the diligent. We live in a time where most people refuse to take responsibility for their own anointing, or for the fields that are their lives over which they were charged with uprooting the thorns and the nettles. We are responsible to repent, remove the rocks; we have to break the fallow ground, and then we have to circumcise our hearts. We have to do all these things. The slothful sinner, who is in bondage to his own slothfulness, which itself is a sin, simply will not. The opposite of slothfulness is righteousness. What could be clearer than that? God's attitude towards lazy and idle people, he contrast them with the righteous.

VOID OF UNDERSTANDING

We are told the slothful are void of understanding. They are both ignorant and deceived, for they understand neither their own business nor what is in their spiritual lives. This is an issue that rises to the level of the ruin of their soul. People go to hell because they were too lazy to do the deeds of the kingdom. They were too lazy to close the door to the devil. They were too lazy to do the work to pull the rocks out of the soil of their own hearts and they were too lazy to pull out the weeds or break up the fallow ground, so the true seed, which is the living word of God, could get into the soil in their hearts. They were just too lazy.

To the slothful comes the eternal judgment, for the slothful will find themselves in the place assigned to the wicked. This is a very serious issue. One of the attributes of the righteous is they are courageous, whereas the slothful lack courage. They are fearful not faithful. It takes courage to confess your sins one to another. It takes courage to look at your sin, and to honestly look at the matters of your heart. It takes courage, and it takes faith. And it takes diligence, but the soul of the slothful desires these things but has nothing. And those who are slothful will always have nothing.

They have no spiritual reward and they have no blessing in the natural. They have nothing. But the soul of the diligent shall be made fat, and rich and prosperous. If you see a man who was diligent in all of his ways, he shall stand before kings. If you become diligent in your affairs and diligent regarding the things of the Kingdom, then you will stand before the KING of Kings.

I have had the opportunity to speak around the country, and I have met a lot of people and heard many comments about the Scriptures. A great majority of the time, what I perceive is an incredibly poor understanding of the word of God. People ask questions that reveal an absolute void of any comprehension of the Scriptures. And how is that possible? Why is there such poor scholarship in regards to the word of God? People are slothful; they read the Bible as if they were reading the TV Guide, perusing it casually. The Lord told us to "diligently study the Scriptures to show yourself approved." He meant through hard work, for this is a serious effort that is required. You do not just flip a few pages, and casually read the Bible. I call that "poor scholarship" and it is the one reason all of the false doctrines were able to come within the church, because the church does not know the word of God. They did not study the word, even though they were told, "study to show yourself approved" but that took too much effort for most of the people.

ENTERING THE KINGDOM OF GOD

It turns out; entering into the Kingdom of God requires real effort. Yes, we were freely forgiven through grace, but now that we have been forgiven, the hard work begins. Even as Israel, in the natural, entered the Promised Land only after driving out the Giants. Taking the Promised Land is a picture of what we have to do spiritually and it takes real effort. You have to show up and put in the effort. The slothful never entered the land, no, they all died in the wilderness, for they lacked the courage and faith to believe the Lord in order to actually go and engage the enemy in the battle. Battling the enemy is hard work, for the kingdom of heaven suffers violence and only the violent take it, and that, through force.

> *His lord answered and said unto him, Thou wicked and slothful servant, thou knew that I reap where I sowed not, and gather where I have not sown. Matthew 25:26*

Jesus called the unfaithful, "wicked and slothful servants." The Lord groups the slothful servants together with the wicked. He also says, "cast the unprofitable servants into outer darkness."

> *And cast ye the unprofitable servant into outer darkness: there shall be weeping and gnashing of teeth. Matthew 25:30*

The word for *unprofitable* used in this verse translates as useless or worthless, for these are the servants who did nothing. The servants that were slothful were the ones who were lazy.

> *And we desire that every one of you do shew the same diligence to the full assurance of hope unto the end: That ye be not slothful, but followers of them who through faith and patience inherit the promises. Hebrews 6:11-12*

Show your diligence, eagerness, carefulness, earnestness through your hard work for the King. The word used for *slothful* in the Greek means lazy, stupid, or dull. Rather we are to be profitable servants who through faith inherit the promise. The slothful are a type of unbeliever who can never inherit the promise.

> *Therefore we labor, that, whether present or absent, we may be accepted of him. 2nd Corinthians 5:9*

The word for *labor* in the Greek means striving, studying, and diligently laboring that we may be acceptable to the Lord.

> *I also labor, striving according to his working which works in me mightily. Colossians 1:29*

LABOR IN THE WORK OF THE LORD

The Greek word for *labor* means to feel fatigued, to work hard, and to become weary. Paul was diligent to the point of fatigue. *Striving* with the work of the Lord, and the word means agonize. I agonize, struggle, compete, fight, and I labor fervently. I strive, with all diligence, exerting all effort, and putting everything into it. Paul says, "I labor and I compete and I agonize for his work." Now here is another clue about the eternal covenant, which was a homework assignment given to all of us by the Lord, and it is very important that we all understand and learn the true meaning of the eternal covenant. This is one of the clues, we labor and we strive according to his working in us. The word for *labor* means prompt and diligent effort, to study and labor hard. Make it a point of hard intense focus, so that you could enter into his rest. Jesus's own words speak of the diligent labors which he requires of us:

> *I know your work, and your labor, and your patience, and how you cannot bear those that are evil, and you have tried those that said they were apostles and they are not, and you found them to be liars you found them to be false teachers from the church in Shinar. Revelation 2:2*

"We found them to be liars." Those men who claim to be his apostles, we have found them to be but liars. Jesus himself examines all we do, and to the righteous he says, *"I know thy works."* The word for works means to toil, your deeds, and your labors. The Lord is saying, "I know your deeds" and he speaking to the diligent ones, not the slothful ones and not to the wicked. He is talking to the ones who labor for his kingdom, and the word for *patience* means hopeful endurance, enduring and continuing, and waiting. "I know your labor, I know your pain, I know your trouble, and your weariness as you patiently endure and continue and you labor and strive for the kingdom. And you have born and have had patience for my namesake and you've labored, you've worked, you've been diligent, and not fainted. Nevertheless I have this against you; you have left your first love."

So the Lord has brought a correction, but at the same time he is acknowledging and giving them credit for having labored for the kingdom. He cites their diligence and their hard labors. This is an intense commitment, which the Lord is looking for and not a convenient faith or a civilian type of faith. "Well if I'm not too busy and if there's nothing else, then maybe I'll do some work for the kingdom." Compare that attitude with the commandment that we should love and serve God with all our heart, all our mind and with all of our strength.

> *Remember therefore from where you fall and repent and do the first works. Revelation 2:5*

The Lord is saying, "go back and do the work you did at the beginning." But he is not speaking to the slothful, for they never worked at all. He is speaking to the diligent. Revelation 2:7 says,

"To him that overcomes I will give to eat of the tree of life which is in the midst of the paradise of my God." And the word for overcome is to conquer, to prevail to gain the victory, to achieve the conquest, to have success.

> *Strive to enter the straight gate, for many shall seek to enter but will not be able. Luke 13:24*

Notice the difference, the diligent *strive* to enter; and the word used means to agonize, struggle, to compete, to endure and to fight and labor fervently in order to enter in. You give whatever it requires. You do not look at this task and say, "Well if it doesn't require too much effort, maybe I will give it a try." No, you do whatever is required and you do not stop until it is done.

COUNTED AMONG THE WICKED

Notice all of the others, the slothful that are counted among the wicked, and who never enter in, they merely *seek to enter*. The word used for *seek* means to desire, or merely inquire. They are interested in entering in, they look into it a little, and the thought occurs to them, maybe they might want to enter in, but that is about as far as it goes. "I looked into that narrow way thing at one point and I thought about it."

Compare that to those who are agonizing, and you will find the difference between those who are being saved and those that will perish on that day. The many to which the Lord is going to say, "I never knew you", they thought about entering in, and they thought they knew him, but they thought wrong. The ones that really know the Lord are the ones who are agonizing and striving to enter in and they do so with all of their hearts. The straight and narrow gate is a place of contest and a fight, where entering in requires a battle, and the Lord told us so in Matthew 7:13 when he said, "Enter by the straight gate, for wide is the gate and broad is the way that leads to destruction, and many there be that go there in because strait is the gate and narrow is the way that leads to life and few there be that find it."

The word for *straight* means a narrow way with obstacles standing close around it. Strait is the gate but it has obstacles around it, and *narrow* means suffering, tribulation, trouble, affliction and the word for *way* means the road or the journey. Strait is the gate. The entrance to the kingdom of life is *very narrow*. It has obstacles in the way, and this journey that leads to life is one of suffering, affliction and tribulation full of trouble.

You are going to have to learn to resist, to strive and to struggle; while you endure the hardships of agony as you begin to master what it means to exercise due diligence. If you are slothful about your salvation, and you approach the things of God with a casual attitude, and you do not want to work very hard, then all that will be left for you is the broad way which leads to destruction. You will be comforted though, for many will be found with you, as the vast majority are all taking the easy way out, passing by the cross, and going the way that seems right in their eyes, putting forth a little effort, for many merely seek to enter, but they will not strive to enter. They may desire it, and even inquire to see if they can find the narrow way, but when they realize this will require real effort because there are obstacles in the way, they give up, because they were not interested in agonizing, they were only interested inquiring.

ONLY A FEW SHALL ENTER IN

There are some that enter in, and they are the "little flock" of the Father. The Scripture calls them the "few" and the word for *few* means very few or very small and few in number. Actually, the definition means only a remnant, whereas the many, they all desire to find an easier way. The word for *many* is *polis* and it means the vast majority, or most of them, the largest group, and the most common. The vast majority who proclaim the name of Jesus, and many have come in his name in this hour, saying Jesus is the Christ, yet they have deceived many, because they are not striving to enter through the narrow gate, they are all looking for an easier way.

There is an easy way, you can join the church in Shinar and there are a thousand different versions of the same basic deception, where they will teach you anything from Hinduism to how to receive the Kundalini anointing but none of this is of the Lord. You can go anywhere you want; you are just not going on the King's Highway. You are going to find out you were actually being driven by the butcher to the slaughter house. Only the holy remnant is actually being led by the Good Shepard, while the many, which only do what is right in their own eyes, are all driven on by the butcher, and many on that day will be slain.

This issue of slothful versus diligent is the issue of our salvation. It is the issue of our life. The many that go down the wide road to destruction, do so because it is more attractive. What allures the multitude is the fact that it is so wide, and it is so broad, and there is room for many different travelers, and many different interpretations and many varied convictions with so many versions of the truth, and all the cults are there, and all of the false religions too, as well as all of the apostate churches from Shinar. The Pharisees walked on that road, and their descendants stand there today. The world is also there, along with all of the multitudes that are perishing.

Why are they so comfortable on the wide road? First, you have an abundance of liberty in this way, that gate is wide open to tempt those who enter therein, and they can go on following after whatever they choose. You can go through this gate with any lie inside of you, and you do not have to repent, so you do not have to agonize. You do not have to endure the dark night of the soul; you can keep your sin and have salvation too. There is no check in your spirit, no measure of your loss, no correction to your character, no condemnation of your sin, and there is no mourning and weeping therein for the world rejoices. The true saints all weep and mourn, while the world yet rejoices.

ON THE WIDE ROAD TO DESTRUCTION

Those on the wide road rejoice as well, for there is no fasting required; you can feast and fill your belly every day, and fill your life full of its sin. You can serve the god of your passion, and have salvation in your imagination, but you will be walking down the wide road to ruin. You can go in the way that seems right in your eyes, seeking the desires of your own heart, confirmed by the many that are there with you. For it is a broad way and there is nothing there to hedge you in, no obstacles to avoid, so you can wander endlessly in any direction, for on the broad way there are many paths within. You always have a free choice, of whatever sin you choose, but all the paths on this road lead to the same end. There is great comfort on the broad way, for there is little to no persecution there, rather you will have the acceptance of the world, and the company of the many who go with you through that wide gate.

You will be following the multitudes, who call evil good and good evil, but in that crowd, you will be going the wrong way, but it is the natural way. It is the easy way and the slothful and the sluggers find a path of ease on this broad way.

It places no great demand on you, there is no striving and no agony, you simply gradually go downhill, walking down easy street to hell. There is no cross to confront you, and no death to the flesh demanded of you, because you are not going to heaven with the little flock, you are going with the many who are perishing who have thrown all caution to the wind.

That, which should frighten you, actually leads you further onto destruction. Eternal death is at the end of this road and all along the way, the power of sin entices you till the end which is everlasting destruction. Whether it be the path of open blasphemy and profanity, or the back way with its closet hypocrisy and hidden sin, it is the exact opposite of the way of holiness. In the way of holiness you are constrained for you must pass through a gate that is straight and both conversion and repentance are required to enter that gate for it is the only way in. And you must go through the cross. You must go through Jesus who is the door in order to begin a new life in him, and to begin to be conformed to true godliness that you might come out of the sin, unbelief, and slothfulness into the state of grace. It is through determination unto righteousness through which we are born again. It requires strength. It is hard to find and even harder still to get through.

Like a passage between two rocks, not only must there be a new heart and a new spirit within you, but the old things must be done away with. That which had corrupted the soul must be changed or discarded. Old habits that corrupted your mind must be forsaken and old customs broken off. What we have been doing all of our days must be undone. We must swim against the tide, and there will be much opposition to your struggle and much resistance from the evil one, with condemnation, mocking, ridicule and persecution from the world without, and from within the false church within.

NARROW IS THE WAY

Is it not clear to see why the slothful and the sluggers cannot and will not enter in? Only those who are diligent and determined to pay whatever cost is required can tread this ancient path which is called *the narrow way*. It is easier to set a man against the entire world than to set a man against himself, yet this is what is required in our conversion at the straight gate, for we must bow down or we cannot enter in at all. We must become as little children and our high thoughts must be brought down. We must deny ourselves, put off the world and its carnal mind, put off the old nature, and be willing to forsake all, for the sake of winning Christ.

The gate is straight and it is blessed of God, it is also not shut but it will be shortly. It is defined as a narrow way because the body must be brought under control, and its corruptions mortified. If your eye causes you to sin, pluck it out. Daily temptation must be resisted, your duty to what is right must be executed and your resistance to what is wrong must be to the death. It requires the exercise of due diligence at all times. You must endure the hardness of the rejection of the world, and you must wrestle and be in agony to overcome your flesh. You must watch all things and walk with care and circumspection and you must pass through much tribulation on the road to the kingdom. You will be afflicted and hedged about with thorns, but God will be with you. But only the diligent will walk therein.

Those that are slothful, who prefer their ease, will all turn away at the first sign of difficulty. The gate is so straight and the way is so narrow, it is not strange that there only a few who find it. And even fewer who choose it and thus enter in. Many who passed by, turned away through their own carelessness. Others look upon it but shun it, not willing to be so limited and constrained. For those that are actually going to heaven are but a few, compared to the vast multitudes of humanity who are all marching into an eternal hell.

The remnant, who are the true chosen of the Father, are but a little flock. Like the gleanings in the vineyard after the harvest, or the eight that were saved in the ark. What discourages so many is that it is a solitary walk. The righteous, rather than turning away, walk on enduring the hardship, embracing the cross. Even though we are but a few, we must press on. No matter the cost, we must continue on with the Lord to the end of all that is of the flesh. And we are required at times to put away our comforts, for the precious prize of winning the true heart of God. We are required to repent and humble ourselves, that we may be exalted in due time. We are required by the Lord to fast and pray and to forsake the entertainment of this hour and to crucify the desires of our flesh, in order to receive the true desire of the kingdom. Yes, the gate is straight and the way is indeed narrow, but the price of heaven and the prize of Jesus make all the effort worth it. We were bid to enter in the straight gate, and it is truly stated that is a matter of life and death. It is a matter of good over evil, and this choice is set before us. To the diligent and to the obedient are the rewards of the kingdom. To the slothful, the lazy and to those that are not willing to pay the price, or not willing to pick up their cross, the wide road is their only other choice.

Enter in by the straight gate, brothers and sisters while there is still time, and while the way is still open, seek him while you may still find him. True conversion is hard work; repentance and humbling yourself requires hard effort. Seeking the Lord with prayer and fasting is hard work, but it is not beyond us if we strive. It is not impossible if we strive. This is it, the time has come, and the choice is yours.

THE JUDGMENT IN THE HOUSE OF THE LORD

Our country is on the verge of a total collapse, and that fact is evident anywhere you care to look, and has been confirmed many times. God's judgment has first come upon the fortress of imagination in the minds of men, but it is ending soon. The breaking of the staff of bread, which is the economy, is almost over. The Lord began his judgment on our economy, but that is only the first judgment, and that judgment will be brought to completion soon. What will follow next is the judgment on the people themselves, and most people are not ready for the second judgment, for this is when the wild beasts shall come into our land.

Son of man, when the land sins against me by trespassing grievously, then will I stretch out mine hand upon it, and will break the staff of the bread thereof, and will send famine upon it, and will cut off man and beast from it: Though these three men, Noah, Daniel, and Job, were in it, they should deliver but their own souls by their righteousness, saith the Lord GOD. If I cause noisome beasts to pass through the land, and they spoil it, so that it be desolate, that no man may pass through because of the beasts: Though these three men were in it, as I live, saith the Lord GOD, they shall deliver neither sons nor daughters; they only shall be delivered, but the land shall be desolate. Or if I bring a sword upon that land, and say, Sword, go through the land; so that I cut off man and beast from it: Though these three men were in it, as I live, saith the Lord GOD, they shall deliver neither sons nor daughters, but they only shall be delivered themselves. Ezekiel 14:13-18

The judgment outlined in Ezekiel 14, comes upon a nation that has sinned grievously against God, and in which the land itself has become defiled. The first judgment is upon the economy, the breaking of the staff of bread. The second judgment is upon the people themselves, as wild beasts come into the land. The word for *wild beasts* translates as an evil company of men who begin the persecution of people. "I will cause noise some beasts to pass through the land and spoil it so that it may be desolate and that no man may pass through on account of the wild beast." There will be no more free passage in the land, no; the interstates will be closed, because of the wild beast. The word for noisome[68] is רעה *ra'ah* and it means evil. Evil beasts are coming. And the word for beast actually translates as a company of men, or troops. An evil company of troops are coming, and they will bring the people to repentance quickly, for when the judgment is in the earth, the people will learn righteousness. Righteousness is coming, quickly, when the evil company of troops come, and they pass through the land, and spoil it, and the word for spoil means to lose your children, and when the evil troops come, they are going to take your children.

It means to lose your children, so that the land shall become desolate and an astonishment, and so that no man may pass through. There will be no more free travel because the lock down is coming, through the evil company of men that are coming. They are going to take your families, they are going to take your freedom and they are going to take your children. This is coming. I think it is time, we got diligent about the word of God and that we diligently seek the Lord.

> *For thus hath the Lord said unto me, Go, set a watchman, let him declare what he sees. And he saw a chariot with a couple of horsemen, a chariot of asses, and a chariot of camels; and he hearkened diligently with much heed: And he cried, A lion: My lord, I stand continually upon the watchtower in the daytime, and I am set in my ward whole nights. Isaiah 21:6-8*

The Scripture says, "Go and set a watchman, and let him declare what he sees." And the prophet responded saying, "I hearkened with much ***diligence,*** and I was in my ward all night, and I still am in the watchtower all day." These are people who are responding with much diligence, for they are responding with everything they have. This is an hour in which we need to respond with everything we have. Not like the slothful, who only do what is convenient.

God has a way of getting our attention, and in this hour, he is sending a noisome company of wild beasts and they are coming in this land after the dollar collapses. I am not a prophet, so do not direct your anger at me. I am just a watchman. I am repeating to you what I have heard and seen. I am giving you a little insight. The Lord has called for prayer and fasting in this hour, and I can tell some of you are responding.

We all must respond, for we all need to be empowered by his Holy Spirit that we could continue more and more to the tearing down of strongholds, and bring every thought and imagination into captivity to the obedience of Jesus Christ. To those who have not yet responded to the cry from heaven, I would encourage you, there is a tremendous blessing in the obedience to the Lord.

The Lord has never once asked us to do something that was bad for us. When the Lord commands you to do something, it is because you need to do it, and it is for your blessing. In this hour, fasting from food as part of your prayer is mandatory, and the blessings that come are tremendous. Fasting and prayer is a game changer spiritually. If you are struggling with depression, anxiety or fear over what is coming, you should begin fasting and praying. If you don't know what to do, then do a long term fast drinking only distilled water which has been steeped in cut up vegetables (celery, carrots, and beets).

A TIME TO FAST AND PRAY

If you have never fasted before, or if you have tried and it has been really hard so you struggled with fasting, the distilled water fast is so powerful. The first three days, yes you will be hungry. I have found that hunger is more for the lust of food than actual hunger. It is more the pleasure of eating, than actual hunger, but we wrestle with it.

What I find most effective, in those times when your flesh is screaming at you, especially if you are preparing dinner for your spouse or your children while you are fasting, as your flesh is screaming, you need to answer your flesh and tell it, "Flesh, you have been crucified with Christ. You are now dead. You have no right to an opinion and I don't want to hear from you again. Get back in the ground and get back in the grave and shut up; you are not going to tell me what to do. You are my servant, and I will command you." Then your flesh will respond, because you have the authority over your own flesh, provided you exercise it. Then go into your prayer closet and pray, "Father who art in heaven, holy is your name, give me this day, my daily bread. Father, please provide for me the living manna that comes down from heaven. The only bread I have to eat today is the living manna that comes from you. If you do not feed me, then I am not eating today. I don't live by the bread of the flesh, but by every word that proceeds out of the mouth of my God."

Go in your prayer closet while you are fasting and praying and ask your heavenly Father for living manna then watch what he does. You will be very excited brethren because the Lord will respond. If you are struggling with the issues of the kingdom, this fast is a game changer. It will overthrow the mind of the flesh and set you free. Quite simply, it is obedience to the commandment of the Lord in this hour. And whenever we obey the Lord, we receive a blessing from the Lord. I would encourage all of you, begin fasting and praying. If some of you have a medical condition so you cannot do a complete fast, or so you believe, then follow the Daniel fast, where Daniel fasted for three weeks eating only fruit and vegetables abstaining completely from meats and bread and all pleasant things. No cookies, no cakes, no crackers, no chips, no soda, no candy and no garbage, only healthy vegetables and fruit for three straight weeks and you will find that is a real fast as well.

While you are fasting, you should also sanctify the time, and turn off the entertainment from Babylon, and get into the worship of the Lord, seek his face in prayer. Study the word. Encourage yourself and your family and friends with songs in Scripture and seek his face with all your heart, because that is all we can do right now. Hard times are coming dead ahead. Whether they come in the next few months or over the next few years, what difference does it make really? We need to be ready for the hour of testing, because when it begins, there will be no chance to make ready then. And the truth is most of us are simply not ready. Why do we care to debate the issue of when? We need to be focused on whether or not we are ready, because these days are coming; they have been prophesied to come, and it was given to us to be the people who would walk through this hour.

So whether they come sooner or later, they are surely coming and we must find ourselves walking in the narrow way. Whatever time is left, we should be redeeming it, to make ready, because only a small remnant is going to be saved from what is coming and most of the church is going to be purified in the fire, while most of those who name the name of Jesus are going to find themselves utterly lost for eternity.

Be encouraged and do the things the Lord is asking us to do and you are going to be fine. Become diligent, like the Bereans in this hour, and rebuke that slothful spirit, for that came right out of hell to disarm and disable us. We do not need that in the camp of the Most High any longer. I would encourage you to begin fasting and praying even now.

Thank you for taking the time to read the second volume of the *Search the Scripture* series. The third volume, *The Remnant shall Return,* shall come forth shortly, for this matter of the King is urgent and of great importance, so that His servants could be warned and instructed, for the time of testing shall soon begin.

God bless you all.

Please remember me in your prayers.

Benjamin Baruch

BE STILL AND WAIT

In darkness there is light

Hope where there is none

A healing heart and a gentle touch

Where there is fear, there lays courage

And answers that will soon be heard

In moments of weakness

When the Lion roars

Be still and wait

For the eagle soars

Reprinted by permission

Marla Eve, January 2015

FOOTNOTES

[1] Job 33:14-15

[2] Job 1:3

[3] Job 1:8

[4] Job 1:13

[5] Job 1:21-22

[6] Job 2:5

[7] Job 3:3

[8] Isaiah 32:1

[9] Job 3:4

[10] Job 3:5

[11] Joel 2:6

[12] Job 3:9

[13] Isaiah 13:10

[14] Job 3:20-22

[15] Revelation 9:6

[16] Job 3:24

[17] Job 4:5

[18] Job 4:7

[19] Job 5:27

[20] Isaiah 48:10

[21] Isaiah 63:9

[22] Mark 13:19

[23] Deut 4:30

[24] Genesis 17:3

[25] Numbers 16:4, Joshua 5:14, Ezekiel 1:28, Daniel 8:17

[26] Matthew 17:6

[27] Matthew 26:38-39

[28] Genesis 49:17

[29] Isaiah 28:13

[30] Psalm 74:14

[31] Luke 1:80

32 Desert G2048, ἔϱημος, erē mos, *er'-ay-mos, lonesome,* that is, by implication *waste*: desert, desolate, solitary, wilderness.

[33] Exodus 3:2

[34] Isaiah 43:19

[35] Exodus 7:16

[36] Proverbs 21:19

[37] Song of Solomon 8:5

[38] Psalm 74:16

[39] Psalm 74:18

[40] 1 John 4:1

[41] https://www.youtube.com/watch?v=vRTDA1F8IkE

[42] Ezekiel 3:15

[43] Ezekiel 13:10

[44] Ezekiel 13:13-14

[45] Ezekiel 13:19

[46] Zechariah 5:4

[47] Deu_25:14

[48] Matthew Henry Commentary on Zechariah 5

[49] *Strange Fire*, by John MacArthur, copyright, 2013. Used by permission of Thomas Nelson. www.thomasnelson.com

[50] John 8:32

[51] Jeremiah 7:4

[52] Cheyne's Isaiah, vol. 1, p. 3

[53] http://biblehub.com/commentaries/daniel/11-32.htm

[54] Matthey Henry's Commentary on the Whole Bible, Jeremiah 9

[55] Proverbs 30:1

[56] http://en.wikipedia.org/wiki/Agur

[57] http://en.wikipedia.org/wiki/Agur

[58] Antiq. II. 6. 1

[59] G. Steindorff ZÄS 27 [1899], 41, 42; ibid., 30 [1892], 50-52

[60] J. Vergote, Joseph en Égypte (1959)

[61] E. Naville JEA 12 [1926], 16-18 See http://www.biblicaltraining.org/library/zaphenath-paneah#sthash.1xOgvIMb.dpuf

[62] International Standard Bible Encyclopedia (1915)

[63] Matthew Henry Commentary on Proverbs

[64] Bear Rule, H4910, מָשַׁל, mashawl, to *rule:* have dominion, a governor, to reign, have power.

---

65 Plain H5549, סלל, salal, *saw-lal,* to *mound* up; to *exalt;* to be exalted and to raise up, plain.

66 Slothful H7503 רפה, raphah, *raw-faw; to slacken*: abate, cease, consume, fail, be faint, be feeble, forsake, idle, leave, let down, be slack, be still, be slothful, be weak.

67 Void H2638, חסר, chaser, *khaw-sare, lacking;* hence *without:* destitute, fail, lack, have need, void, want.

68 Noisome H7451 רעה, ra ah, *raw-aw; bad* or *evil,* evil man, exceedingly great, noisome, sore, sorrow, trouble, vex, wicked, worst wretchedness, wrong.

Made in the USA
San Bernardino, CA
26 September 2016